TRACKING THE PREDATOR: THE AFTERMATH OF SEPTEMBER 11, 2001

A CANADIAN WOMAN SPEAKS

BY

SANDRA C. JOHNSTON

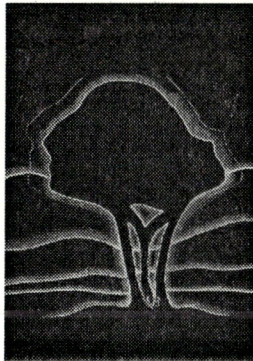

First published by AuthorHouse 05/29/04

ISBN: 1-4184-6284-5 (e-book)
ISBN: 1-4184-3192-3 (Paperback)

Printed in the United States of America
Bloomington, Indiana

This book is printed on acid free paper.

Photo Credits
Cover photo by Leanna Callum
Author photo and cover design by Jeremy Gregson
Illustrations by Verena Blackbird

ACKNOWLEDGEMENTS

...for all my relations great and small
...for all those who have gone before to inspire and enthuse me

The Honourable Jean Chretien
Jean Shinoda Bolen
Joan Borysenko
Deepak Chopra
Wayne Dyer
Clarissa Pinkola Estes
Matthew Fox
Carolyn G. Heilbrun
Jean Houston
Alice Miller
Starhawk
Marianne Williamson
Marion Woodman

And many other great thinkers and writers who have had the courage to tell it like it is.

My gratitude to Verena Blackbird and Patricia Sword, native Canadians and my sisters in spirit, who have walked with me on many forked trails and have taught me the importance of assimilation with discretion.

Thank you Jeremy for your responsible stewardship and being a co-creator in my life.

To Betty Clark whose courage through so many losses has inspired me to go through the fire of transformation.

To my good friends, Judy Doher and Patricia Stockwell, for working beside me for so many years.

Author's Note: There are published versions of Bluebeard in the collections of Johan and Wilhelm Grimm, Charles Perrault, Henri Pourrat and others.

DEDICATION

To my father, 1ˢᵗ Lieutenant William Frederick McNear of the Royal Canadian Regiment, who served his country on the front lines in World War II.

He went to war at the age of seventeen and engaged in combat in the Hitler Line, Gustavline and Gothic Line. His theatres of war included Africa, France, Belgium, Holland and Italy. He took a sniper's bullet in the face in the Gothic Line at Rimini Airport, Italy.

My father went off to serve his country as a strong, athletic young man full of vim, vigour and courage defending not only his nation but the nations of the free world. He returned home wounded, shell-shocked and chronically anxious with high blood pressure and unresolved grief over the loss of his own vital life and the lives of his young friends and comrades who were wounded or killed beside him.

"I arrived in England via New York and was immediately directed to training troops because, by this time, I was schooled in Canada as a well-trained, qualified instructor. I served in this capacity until August and volunteered for service in Africa as part of the reinforcements for the R.C.R.

We traveled from Britain to Canada, south to the equator, to the strait of Gibraltar in North Africa and into the Mediterranean. This was to avoid the German submarines in the North Atlantic ocean. There were one hundred and fifty ships with approximately seven thousand men aboard each of them in the convoy. The seasickness was terrible; the men could hardly stand the smell of food let alone eat it. The Germans hit us with torpedo planes off the coast of Italy and we lost twenty-nine ships. Many others were hit including mine. The compartments of the ship were completely sealed off to prevent it from flooding and sinking if it was hit. One hundred and fifty-five men died in one of those compartments, one of them being my very good friend. It was very hard to bear.

I was in charge of thirty-nine soldiers and was not in favour of being sealed below deck in a raid so we found an area topside to wait it out unseen. It was survival.

The attack was launched from Africa into Sicily and then into Italy. After two days of battle, the Italians capitulated and left the Germans to face us. We fought right up to the Po Valley, enduring many hardships, casualties and fighting experiences. We established a static front for three months in Ortona where it rained every day. We began to call it the land of "liquid sunshine".

We attacked on Christmas Eve and, while crossing a trench, I was blasted by an explosion nearby and suffered a concussion. The shock and stress of that blast landed me in the hospital where I nearly died of pneumonia.
When I was sent back to my division, we were ordered to attack Rimini Airfield. I kept my men back while the points entered the buildings in search of the enemy. Since they drew no fire, I started across the vineyards and was hit in the face by a sniper located on top of a silo. Where the bullet entered my cheek, the hole was no larger than the tip of my little finger but, where it exited my neck, the hole was as big as my fist. I had to hide in the silos for nearly five hours while we secured the area. I managed to escape downhill to an ambulance while we were still under fire.
By the time I recovered, the war was drawing to an end so I was re-assigned to Belgium and Holland where I was in transportation until the Armistice was declared. My nerves broke on the ship home and I would never be the same again.
I could not possibly begin to describe the experiences I had in the service. There were some good times; other times it was horrifying. The travel and the camaraderie were the good parts; the battles and the loss of friends

and so many good young men come back as haunting memories now. I try not to remember but, the older I get and unable to stay busy, I am flooded at times with sadness and regret".

The casualties in the Italian campaign totaled 92,757 of which a quarter were Canadians. The young Canadians who died numbered 5,764. There were 19.486 wounded and 1,004 captured.

LEST WE FORGET!

*The strategy of the Germans made no sense; they **lost much more than they gained**. We must remember!*

To my grandmothers and grandfathers and to my mother, Marie Ryan McNear. The grieving at home was the worst part of the war.

To all who suffered the loss of their sons and daughters in all past and current wars and conflicts.

May we move out of the "War Zone" and not have to study war anymore.

TABLE OF CONTENTS

PART I

FORWARD

As a culture, we are in a mythic time and place. This is truly a time of "liminality" – of passage from one stage of living to another. When we venture psychologically out beyond the "known world", we are heeding a call to live more authentically. This movement into unfamiliar terrain will always cause conflict and uncertainty but it is the pain that can only lead to more conscious evolution and responsible living on both the personal and collective level.

When we can stop long enough to begin to formulate questions, we show a maturity of thought, desire and action. It is a sign of growing up and moving out of unacceptable systems of thought, manipulation and power.

Significant mythic journeys always begin at a juncture when exceptional circumstances initiate an heroic response. The call brings up the curtain on a mystery of transfiguration – a spiritual passage which, when completed, amounts to a dying and a birth. The familiar life has been outgrown and the old concepts, ideals and emotional patterns no longer fit.

I believe that the time of the passing of a threshold is at hand. The question is, who is courageous enough to heed the call and has the right "stuff" one is made of, the soul, to meet the challenges and losses on the journey. This is never for the faint of heart. It takes integrity to step through and go beyond the known world. This is the crucifixion – conscious suffering of the "slings and arrows" that will be wielded by those stuck in traditional ways of being that no longer have meaning.

Will **you** be able to step through with me as I take you on a journey to discover your wisdom and truth or will you hide your eyes with shame and continue to rationalize the lies of hand-me-down thought and value systems that do not always have our best interests at heart? These systems may have been useful at a certain time or in a certain place but may be anathema now to the only constant which is change.

What will **you** allow to die in order to bring new life. I ask you…

Where?

Where will this journey lead?
Where did it begin
that desperation fear and loneliness
that haunt her still?
How does she sustain?
When will it lift
that depression?
Where will she find relief?
Orphaned now…martyr then
senseless pain…no respite
An old order haunts
Never lurks and joy is vague

AT WHAT COST?

The world is full of fear. We need a paradigm shift both within our inner worlds and, ultimately, in the outer world.

What kind of power can propel us beyond the present personal – particular focus of local life to the universal realm?

Will our awakening come in time?

Killing Mother

Prostrate in a broken world
Riddled from abuse and toil
Reclused, unsanctioned and spoiled,
a cold earth scorns her design
An old order chants: "I told you so".
Debris abounds, a dirty life
bigotry, hatred and the rage is
masked by splendid paint.
A howling fierce untimely yet
carves respite in her bones.
A starving orb
and tainted river
refuse, neglect and pain
pretend regret
for an anointed time
of black and gold and red

PROLOGUE

A THRESHOLD–

AN INVITATION

This is a very spiritual time. The veils of illusion are thinning. We are at a threshold – a concept which is as old as time

Threshold moments can be thrust upon us as were the events of September 11, 2001 in the United States and they can represent a new starting point. Crossing a threshold invites stepping into new territory, unfamiliar terrain.

The challenge to awaken to the truth of our lives invites feelings of anger, fear, anticipation, excitement and anxiety. It can feel like a very painful time. This pain is the pain of becoming more fully alive ..if we choose; alive to our fullest potential as gifted human beings.

This pain is truly a crucifixion – a conscious suffering. This is Christ-consciousness and not about martyrdom.

This leads to personal ascension in terms of greater self-actualization. Whenever we have the courage to move forward into greater consciousness, we are bringing others with us. The path is made by walking. We are truly "in crisis". This is Calvary and we have just begun the climb.

Can we make the events of September 11, 2001 sacred; cultivate and deepen our awareness that it was indeed a threshold moment? I believe the world is being invited to step out of ordinary time and to experience mystery ... an opening to the deeper truths of our lives.

There will be no magical solution.

A NECESSARY DEATH-

EXPLORING TERRAIN

In the midst of what is being considered the worst of man's inhumanity to man, the question most asked is "where is Osama Bin Laden?"

I say that he is alive and well and that he stands almost indestructibly in this place and time. I also believe that unfortunately, dead or alive, he is insidiously present everywhere in our world.

Some of you have undoubtedly heard of the concept of "living the question."

I believe the question we must now live in the meantime is: "where are we going"?

We are truly at a threshold which is not just about going through, but also about opening and creating space to receive. Perhaps we have been brought to a necessary death in terms of what was or what used to be, economically, militarily, religiously and politically. What has been our focus and intent for so many centuries is no longer working.

We are entering a sacred time, out of ordinary time and space. We must become open, receptive, and yielding. It is time for paying attention…we must not go to sleep.

I am writing as a woman raised in Patriarchy, which is a politic about "control over". I have lived and died many times to many things. I bear the scars of my courage on my body, in my heart, in my mind and on my bank account. I am weary. I speak to you from the wisdom of lived experience.

Lost Call

I held the space and spread the news
to the circle that came round
I spark the flame and fan the sage

and holiness abounds

As moisture comes to wet the task
I move deeper in
I chant and pray and invoke the gods
begging peace from within

The coffer is not in sight
only totems, signs and song
I signed bankruptcy papers today
and wonder what went wrong

I followed priests and read the psalms
I held my hands in prayer
I listened long and studied hard
now I sit here in despair

What promises went down in vain
to bring my deepest song
My spirit's strong, my body weak
where do I belong?

Am I born before my time
or in the after all?
I miss reminders of better days
when I could hear a holy call

I am told that there were women when
on altars they stood stern
in their command of speech and love
in bodies round and firm

Could I have been one of them
in faith and in deep knowing?
I need refreshment and renewal now
to keep my embers glowing

THE DARKEST TIME IS JUST BEFORE DAWN-
THE PROBLEM

Over and over again we have seen madmen rise to great power. How could this happen? What creates such a need for demi-gods and such acceptance of their power and blind obedience to their rules? Blind faith comes to mind and personal emptiness. Have we become automatons, "robotized" and duped over and over again by those who said they had "our best interests" at heart? This hunger for truth needs to be explored, named and exposed.

Maybe it's time that we discover at a deeper level, what our best interests really are so that we might become more flexible and trusting of our instincts in order to take better care of ourselves.

There is such rigidity in our thinking. It manifests in our bodies, minds and spirits as aridity or dryness. We might ask: "How do we bring more moisture into our lives?". It may be our tears that have already started which will begin the dance of intimacy at a personal and collective level. We are a world in mourning and the darkest time is just before the dawn.. We cry because we want something better.

We are almost at a point in history when we need to teach ourselves to be human again. We live disconnected from self, others, the Earth, and the Creator. We need a template for healing our spiritual and creative malaise.

The horrors of September 11, 2001 in New York City have awakened every culture at some level to the evil lurking within the psyches of humankind. These atrocities have been called crimes against innocents. I believe that these monstrous attacks are a replication of a long line of murderous activities committed for centuries in the name of God.

The question arises in my heart. "Who is this God who chooses to keep men and women with their thoughts on heaven, hell and the hereafter rather than on the present, this world, and our place in it?" Our lives and our world have been given to us for learning and evolving in mind, body and spirit. Now we have suicide bombers. How could any force calling itself divine, prefer barrenness to fruitfulness? It seems a terrible betrayal to the creative forces that gave life to the world.

Distortion

The words seep out
"boxed constricted torn
abnegated oppressed"
I am weary from the pain
and the toil that held
no promises
"More joy in heaven"
he said from the pulpit
and then gave communion
from an altar that I
had cleaned that day
"Prepare for the Lord
say only the Word and
you shall be healed"
Mea culpa…mea maxima culpa
Through my most grievous fault
Therefore I beseech Thee
O Lord The pain of the
knowing The rage from the
remembering The scars
from the living death
keep a tight hold on me
Forgiveness is not
in the forgetting but
in the full remembrance
I will let it go

Poetry is the language of the feminine energies within every man and woman. It speaks to us if we would only listen, of a knowing down and deep within each of us. This is the terrain that I suggest we open to exploring, not with fear and distaste, but rather, with excitement and awe.

The images, metaphors, cadences, and music that come through as we map this territory can help us to contain and understand our very existence. When our personal experiences begin to match this wisdom, our personal truth naturally "bubbles up" from within us. How empowering!

This is about spiritual practice and there is no place for dogma here. The process involves using a journal in order to ground one's thoughts, praying for grace to walk the path of higher consciousness, meditation to stay centered in Self knowledge, and listening most especially to our bodies which have often been left out of the ascent towards wholeness and deeper wisdom. I speak here about knowledge that comes from living and learning - a "process" oriented approach, the way of the healthy feminine instincts, the way that brings the union of thought and living.

THIS IS TRUTH AND I DARE YOU!–

THE EMERGENCE OF "POWER OVER"

A long, long time ago the Goddess in her many forms was worshipped on many places on Earth and was eventually destroyed. She had been a representation of the sacredness of life made manifest. She did not represent female rule over man but rather, freedom from rule. That was a time of Earth – based spirituality. The intrinsic worth of each individual was acknowledged. Each person's truth and emotions were respected and resistance was not judged and the process of individual change was seen to proceed at its own pace.

As I write, I can hear the male voices of the experts on CNN who seem to be responsible for most of the decisions concerning the recent terrorists attacks. There seem to be few female reporters and many anchormen.

For thousands of years there has been no feminine face of the Creator. It used to be that women were leaders and priestesses, revered members of society. It was a time when women had power. "Power-over" had not yet been institutionalized. There was little evidence of structures of domination, no evidence of images of war, kings and conquests.

With the growth of cities in early societies came the concept of centralized power. This was the beginning of the changes that would wrestle power from women and most men. Short term war lords were elected to face sporadic external threats which set the precedent for the eventual election of kings. Warfare became more common. The concept of kingship and make rule were imposed by patriarchal conquerors in Indo-Europe. Culture and the human personality became restructured in the image of domination, a "power-over" dynamic.

Consider that the transition to Patriarchy was the maximization of power-over. It seemed that every change of political power represented a new stage in the transition to a hierarchical, patriarchal, militarist society.

I do not pretend to be an historian but I do encourage you to explore the truth of my tenet that women's power eventually eroded completely through changes in laws, religious practices, records of customs, and transactions and myths in history books that carry "herstory".

What am I really saying? I will attempt to give language to a concept that is difficult to explain because it is just beginning to emerge and make itself known. Its presence is sneaking in the back door. As a therapist, I see it in rampant addictions, eating disorders, relationship problems, depression, anxiety, and suicide. The forgotten feminine is struggling to be acknowledged. (The feminine energies that reside in each man and each woman are aching to be recognized). Where and when there is a/any problem, there is separation. (Our feminine is separated off, isolated, in hiding and yearning to get out). It is my belief that the escalation of current terrorism has much to do with disrespect for feminine "feeling" values (in all men and women) that are dominated by rational thought. I am not being gender specific because all of us, both men and women, have been affected by the loss of this part of us that represents the feminine face of God.

Disillusioned

It was the heart start
of a long affair
Shadow Prince Maiden Fair
coming together in time
of need
and fear
demanding relief
he from her
as mother source
she from him
as father care
it was a blending
a fusion feeling rare
in remembered time
Life intervened
there was so much
to sort
so much carried
out of fear and sanctity
Lost son and daughter

from another time
of knowing

THE REQUIRED RENAISSANCE-

THE GODDESS IS RAGING

The male phallic symbols, the twin towers of the World Trade Center of New York City have been bombed and have crumpled upon the sleeping giant and super power, the United States of America. I am Canadian, a sister in spirit of her neighbour, the U.S.A. Canada has often been accused of being too quiet. Our land has not been ravaged by terrorist attacks but we are not exempt in terms of a required renaissance.

I have heard it said that tyrants can become our greatest teachers. Are we willing to pay attention to what is really in front of us? This horrific attack of terrorism is a wake - up call. It is the "fait accompli" which might propel us towards greater personal and collective evolution.

In being wounded from this tragedy, our souls and psyches are opened up. New questions begin to be formulated about who we really are in our depths. We have been wounded and a larger story can be revealed in this wounding. This is a wake-up call for the world.

We have been sleeping through nuclear threat, the "desertification" of the planet, and the mounting evidence of our violence towards one another. We close our eyes to the great beauty of nature around us, the gratuitous generosity of strangers, the delight of the playing child, the extraordinary patterns of the stars in the night sky and the red and gold of happy sunsets. We strive for increased profits at the expense of our families, our bodies and our souls. We strive to get more accomplished in less time. We eat poorly, swallow anti-depressants, rest less and keep going. Where? Why? In our land of abundance we pollute. We are mesmerized by violence at an early age. Did you take time for breakfast? Is dinner with your family a fantasy? Imbalance rules.

In order to bring a renaissance or metamorphosis, we must bring change to our relationship with ourselves, the world, and to our spiritual powers/ forces.

How do we awaken the immortal soul into real time and go beyond fear-based thought forms and insecurities that hide behind acts of power and aggression? What are the clues that point to the necessary awakening and metamorphosis of ourselves? For it is only by beginning with ourselves that we can truly change our world. Cleaning up our own back yard first is critical. Just see how a positive change in the way you speak and behave affects those around you. The ripple effect has tremendous power.

Perhaps we need to learn to pray differently. Perhaps we need to ask for "Deliverance" by the Divine One that Jews, Christians, and Muslims have in common. In the words of Matthew Fox in his book, "The Coming of the Cosmic Christ": "Deliver us Divine One from:

Patriarchy's dualisms (right/wrong, good/bad, either/or, heaven/hell)
Proneness to self pity
Sentimentalism (displays of emotionalism)
Violence
Lack of imagination
Intellectual laziness
Lack of authentic curiosity
Separation of the head from the body
Separation of the body from feelings
Preoccupation with sex
Fear of intimacy with the self and others
Reptilian brain (repetition compulsion)
Anthropocentrism
Crucifixion of Mother Earth
Envy and manipulation of children
Abuse of women
Homophobia
Righteousness
Idolatry of nationhood and national security
The forgetfulness of beauty and art
The impotence to heal
Sadomasochism
Parental cannibalism and devouring children
Lack of balance in our lives
The savaging of the earth
The quest for immortality
Ego
The waste of talent and resources, human and earth
Human chauvinism

*Compulsion to go into debt to finance our bloated lifestyles
Matricide"*

These are the terrors of our time. These are in our faces. The terrorists, in their acts of hatred, have shown how we live and they live in our faces for us to see, to feel, perhaps unwittingly, as an opportunity of sorts.

Perhaps we can sort out what we have lost from what we have gained in the aftermath of such a disaster as September 11, 2001. Perhaps on an individual level as well as a community and a national level, we will begin to think and reassess. Perhaps we will accept that we are not perfect; we are not greater than. We are all really wounded and have been for some time and we had better explore that. Perhaps we need to heal because now, we have truly had to feel.

Feeling has unlocked and unearthed mighty emotions. For the first time many of us have seen powerful and authoritative men openly weep. We have felt what being human feels like.

Old Guard

*The King is dying
The cancer signals
the collapse
of an old order
digging its heels
into nothing but
piss and vinegar
and sugared distemper
Look old man!
See the scabs
on her face
signaling collapse
of internalized order
hideously exposing
itself in open sores
and beads of pus
on a once so
passionate maiden*

17

Scratch your balls
and feel the
limpness of an appendage
that can no longer
shoot for glory
Bed yourself in
the cemetery green
and remember nothing
of the ravages of
your incompetence
and cowardice
in the face of your child
your daughter
who will go to her grave
carrying the scars
of her courage
in the battle of life
dying many times
to your illusions
casting light
on your delusions
to no avail
Fuck your priests
and all the goddamn lunatics
that meet you in
the hallways of
deceit and glorified
triumph in the
Father's heaven
This is a liquid holiness
born of retreat
and withering fortitude
You are master Bastards
defying fate
Death is in your face
and you are
paralyzed by discontent
and collective disarray
It is all part of the game
you say
Well! I do

not have to suffer it!
I will take up
the sword
I challenge
you to a duel
that could make
cowards of us all

THE INFORMATIONAL POTENTIAL OF LOSS-
NAMING THE GAME

It is my belief that, if our thinking and beliefs change, the way we respond to circumstances in our lives will also change. To improve our lives in any way means we must muster up the courage to step into unfamiliar territory non-defensively. Difficult events can catapult us into a sequence of "unfoldments" that could move us toward improvements that we have always said we wanted to make. We must change more than the outer circumstances of our lives. The events of loss open the path to changing ourselves at a very deep level. Inconvenient, yes, but amazingly transformational. The voice of the feminine encourages the path of "unfoldment". After a life-altering event and, when embarked upon, through awareness, grief, willingness, action and struggle, great healing can take place.

Healthy masculine energies that represent responsible stewardship could support these potentially healing discoveries but, our inner Bin Laden energies are about fear-based masculinity in both men and women. This internal psychic predator is not integrated and will wield atrocities against any change like an old king. Platitudes, invectives, old psychic prescriptions and proscriptions will surface and the internal battle is frightening for most. This toxic magician knows just enough about human behaviour to manipulate us back into old familiar ways of operating that really have never and are not serving us. Yes, this energy is alive and well in our individual psyches as well as the collective psyche or unconscious of the whole world. In general, the unconscious here means anything we are not aware of in our being or in the culture.

Because it is so tied to old laws, old rules, and social structures that no longer serve us, this energy terrorizes us into compliance and complacency. We all have within us an inner demand for evolution and an innate design for growth and self development. This internal predatory energy not only stalls and manipulates us in our natural quest for growth, but it acts internally as a living death wish in that regard.

Life becomes very difficult when we operate/behave/conduct our lives with the shadow of our own personal Bin Laden always lurking inside of us. There is a cost involved in resisting our own personal, natural evolution – we become victims of a terrorist within ourselves. When we live outside of this awareness of our own dark energy, when we are simply not aware of it, we will project it out into the outer world onto those who will "contain" it because of their lack of awareness. By containing it, I mean that they take it on as if it were entirely their own. We scapegoat women, children and minority groups most especially. They begin to "act out" or "act in" what is being loaded onto them. Thus we have domestic violence, rampant depression, attention deficit disorders, eating disorders, suicides, homicide, addictions and other reactive problems. We create the O.J. Simpsons and the Bin Ladens of the world through ignorance and irresponsibility for our own darkness.

We have terrorists ready to blow up the world without any definitive cause. They use religious beliefs as a foil. What they are searching for is "power-over". In other words, our patriarchal mind-sets have unconsciously created the Hitlers and Bin Ladens. We have always needed scapegoats. They exist to relieve us of responsibility and accountability for our behaviour.

She Figures It Out

A creative solution to the pain
does not count in the scheme of things
only expected compliancy and reliability
You are to be the one "messed up" flawed
accused of what is already being done to you
Crazy making is what it is – rise up
O daughters of the Patriarchy! Pay heed!
This is double indemnity…do no get close
to naming the game…support the myth
Do not be aware or you will pay with
your cell tissue and your vital life!
This is their mandate You are paying already
Don't you see?

Why is it we need scapegoats? Why do we so often kill the messenger?

We live in an addictive society; its construct is based primarily on shaming, blaming and "'guilting". This has been a way for people to manage internal and external equilibrium. By this I mean that we are so unable to differentiate our feelings as they come up that we only feel tension mounting; ready to blow a side-wall at the least provocation. We try to soothe ourselves with alcohol, drugs, sex, violence and primary relationships. It all serves to keep us busy but we really do not get anywhere. We continue to be indirect instead of being direct in terms of what we really need, want or desire. Half of the time it is because we really do not know and "wheedling" becomes a way of relating. We use sarcasm instead of speaking the truth and tear each other down in order to feel better about ourselves and to control the other by making them second-guess themselves or, we keep them off balance by never letting them know how special they are to us. We are so afraid of feelings that might make us feel vulnerable when we share them.

TRIANGULATION-

THE VICTIM/VILLAIN/RESCUER GAME

We are guilty of engaging in triangulation on an individual and societal level. In the blame game every victim needs a villain in order to manipulate rescue.

It looks like this:

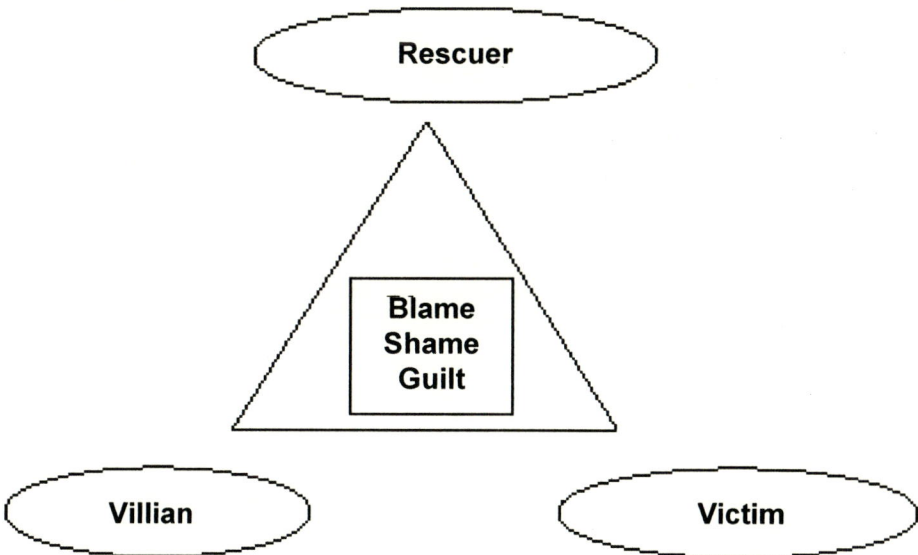

The rescuer's focus here is the victim. The irony here is that the victim wields the most power in that he/she can manipulate the rescuer and blame the villain. The victim is off the hook with his/her "poor me" mentality because he/she is not being responsible or accountable and gives the message covertly or overtly, "If you don't help me I will get you." This is seductive to the rescuer, who, not realizing it, is already two down so to speak. First, he/she is abandoning him/her self in being more "other" directed than "inner" directed. Second, it will be she/he who will be blamed if anything does wrong. **It is a set-up**. This is where "powerlessness" can become the worst evil.

We see this especially in addictive relationships which are the primary addiction in our culture. In the outer world neither person is in control of their internal states. The woman is usually out of touch with her anger and finds a man, who, already out of control of his own anger, will act out hers as well. She has been culturally encouraged as a woman to express fear or sadness or insecurity and not to assert herself. This is the basis of the cycle of violence. The tensions builds up in the man, the woman knows or feels it happening – she will do something to "get his goat" as victim so he will "get it over with" and then the honeymoon stage begins with his remorse and her position of power is established for a short time once again.

This is a "sick-lical" game and it manifests itself in every institution in our culture. It is underscored and constantly inculcated in the basic unit/ structure of our society/culture – the family. This game goes on "within" a person when fear and insecurity take hold. It happens when one tries to make changes but blames oneself for any disruption in the inner or outer world.

The victim part of us is not conscious or aware, the inner tension mounts because of the emotional battle going on that we often have no language for. The villain, dark or unconscious Bin Laden in us will give us a good flogging which will invite our internal rescuer who might say: "There, there it will be alright. Just sleep awhile or have another drink, pop a pill or exercise once again". This dynamic manifests itself in self abuse. Lame excuse for not doing anything about anything is the consequence and the cycle repeats itself. This drug dealer of psychic highs and lows is mighty seductive.

It has become a way of life, expecting others to help maintain our equilibrium (the status quo) because we are out of touch with our own internal states. If we were all less "feeling stupid" and a lot more aware and conscious, we wouldn't be able to tolerate this co-dependency that keeps the game going.

This dynamic is about escape from intimacy (personal, relational, and cultural) and is not co-creative, which is based on compassion and creativity.

When we suffer "consciously" we develop compassion, a greater capacity to "be with" the self and the other and all that lives. The victim/villain/ rescuer dynamic supports victim psychology, behaviour and its shadow - martyrdom. **After all, you can't fault a saint can you?**

Tarnished Angel

She sits and smokes
In a worn out chair
Her eyes are blurred to time
The jaws they curl to fan
the rage as she weaves
her web of lies
Tomorrow leers – a grand display
she misses pain and sorrow
The chalice tips a bitter wine
a gall that burns and blisters
A lip that curls – a raspy voice
chortles songs of dread and fear
The neediness buried deep within
is masked by shaky charm
The cauldron's dry – the witch
holds fire and whips
her into feeble shape
A tarnished soul – a wasted life
toddles off to bed to sleep
the sleep that cuts off dreams
and beckons more disguise

STALKING THE BEAST

There are many predatory energies within the psyches of every human being. If they remain unconscious, they will wreak havoc with our spirits. We all need to bring these predatory energies to the light of consciousness. But, how?

There is what I will call a "complex" which lurks at the edge of all our lives waiting for opportunity to oppose the feminine energies in both men and women. It wants to evict insight, intuition, endurance, deep capacity for loving, keen sensing, far-sightedness and creativity. This is malignant energy which operates in the unconscious; personally and collectively. If one does not become aware, this destructive magician will seduce us into believing it is working in our best interests. It operates insidiously to undermine all feminine aspects of self, other, community and culture. **Does this remind you of anyone?** This is Bin Laden energy and it wants territory.

The energy of the predator within wants superiority and power over others. It is inflated energy that is hell-bent on deflating. It is poison to anything which may bring life-giving/affirming energy to the individual or anyone else. This dark mage is an enemy bent upon disempowering the deep feminine wisdom in each and every man and woman.

Lost

There she was
Blithe spirit
Nuptial virgin
Free as the wind
Song in her heart
What kind of shuffling
led to the scowl
the plodding
round and round deterring wholeness?

THE DARK NIGHT

The dark energy within is something I am on intimate terms with as a psychotherapist and also in my personal life, having been on the other side of the desk in the counselling room. My clients have taught me much through their individual work but I venture to say that most of my insight comes from lived experience. I believe that depression and uncontrollable aggression is rampant in our culture. Most times depression has to do with "involuted" anger meaning anger that is turned inward toward the self. This seems to be the way for many women and some men who are often "too good" for their own good. Aggression, the outward expression of anger, has become the way of most men and some women.

In my own experience of coming to terms with my dark side as well as spending thousands of hours sitting as witness to clients as they do the same, I feel that this period in our time is truly the dark night of the soul. It is the agony in the garden. So many everywhere are suffering, lost, alone and hungry for love.

Up to this point in the business of "doing personal work", which could be called "recovery of the soul", there has been a naivete about this dark energy that has been projected outwards for so long. I come up against tremendous resistance from clients when it comes to the long process of letting go, in a slow release of the stifling executioner within, with its false promise of security. It digs its heels in when it is cornered. When it seems life change may be imminent, a fierce internal battle begins.

Guano Stare

What is this shit?
What is this stuff?
What means it all
in the long run?
in the short run?
in the end?
in the night's beginning?
Where did it start?
When does it stop?

Why did it happen?
When do I drop?
This is a mess
This is such pain
Where did it come from
this panic and rain?
Order from chaos
freedom from pain
Where does it end?
What did I gain?
Freedom from sorrow?
Absence from tears?
Laughter and freedom?
Joy once again?

THE FEMININE ENERGY IN MAN–

DIVING IN

When a child experiences the lack of an "awake" mother, she/he is deprived of her/his connection with her/his own innate knowing and caution. (This loss of normal development of instinct and the corresponding normal trusting of instinct is crucial). It robs the boy of his ability to connect with his natural feminine instinctual knowing. Many men and women with "not-awake" mothers and fathers navigate their world in a semi-somnambulistic state (semi conscious in the real sense of the word). **Many of these people run our educational systems, our country, corporations, and institutions!**

When we remain naïve to the evil energy lurking within, we are doomed to repeat destructive patterns. This Bin Laden energy is a drug dealing energy which makes us want and need (psychic) highs no matter how self defeating. Many people powered by this negative energy end up living less instead of more. They are not able to point their finger at the abuser because of the insidiousness of its presence.

Many men and women have been restrained in early life during the normal gradual periods of the individuation process. This is the process of "leaving home" and forming a separate self which feels entitled to the gifts of the world, who feels loveable, capable, and worthy. They have been restrained by the imperatives "should, ought or must". Many of these adults end up living falsely and feeling empty. They go through the motions of living not really aware. Their feelings overwhelm them. Their murder had been planned from the start by their internal predator for the purposes of aggrandizement and ego inflation.

What is our way out of this?

Our key to awareness is authentic curiosity and the ability to look behind and beyond the veils of illusion with the hooded eyes of the owl. We must be able to peer into the truth and accept the feelings that come with the recognition of having been "robotized" and duped by society's invectives and precepts.

We need to know the deepest, darkest secrets of the psyche; that there is something which degrades us, destroying and inhibiting potential. Injured instincts allow us to fall prey to the promise of pleasure, higher status, never ending love, ease, and increased security.

ENLIGHTENMENT–

YOU DON'T KNOW WHAT YOU DON'T KNOW

There is an innate demand for spiritual evolution within each and every human being on earth. Through addictions of one form or another, we have been able to shut off or suppress this natural yearning of the soul. Our need is to move toward greater consciousness both personally and culturally and give up the idea that we should have, or be entitled to have, everything we need at elbow's length.

In these times of fear or of "threatening decompensation" as I call it, a creative energy is finding room to show itself. As a therapist, I work to provide the "holding environment". I represent a **conscious** mother who can support the very important "empowerment process", whereby the client comes to an awareness of loss of self. This realization begins a grieving and deepening process as a prelude to moving forward. In this capacity as a role model for feminine development, I am able to encourage and support healthy growth and development.

For a man, I am the **conscious** parent supporting him in his discoveries about himself, his family and his world without criticizing or using him as his unconscious mother may have done. It is a frightening time of regression and vulnerability for him as his greatest fears come up for healing. Healing is a process that can only happen when people unearth their own truths - what they truly feel - in a safe environment. This safe environment is the "holding environment" that I spoke of earlier. These awakened feelings have been defended against most of his life and have often been the basis of chauvinism or mysogyny.

Men's feminine energies have been tied to "cultural imperatives" in terms of what a real man should be. These invectives operate within the man as "wicked witch" energy that inhibits the flow of true emotion which is ready and willing to bring him to vital life! Memories of the all- powerful mother upon whom he depended for his very life, surface. Fears of being devoured or abandoned also surface for healing.

At this point in the process of healing, he no longer projects mother onto me as therapist or any other woman because he is getting things straight around **his** mother as he begins to see her in a very different light. As he becomes more and more conscious, he is developing a greater capacity to be with an outer woman (a wife, girlfriend, sister, daughter). In this process too, he has also mourned the lack of male initiation by the father into the ways of men and healthy male development. He is able to see that his father was probably wounded himself and was not able to provide a healthy model for masculine development.

Cruel Priestess

I hate her careless venom
under which pity laps like a flame
crazy making is what it is
How do I orient myself at this
tenuous time when the cord finds
itself in the shreds of time run amuck?
I am an abyss walker and I
am insecure in the scheme of things
This is the price I paid for all
that early daytime success
This was early truth and I
acted my way through it
I cry now for all that was
fought and lost for all
the fathers gone and all
that strength and goodness
I never experienced
for the many mothers
wherever you are

SABOTAGE-

IS IT MARRIAGE?

Many people marry, I believe, because a new status is being sought. Perhaps it is a symbol of maturity and an attempt at completion of necessary individuation from mom and dad. However, without knowing it, they are still tied to the unconscious of their parents. I have heard the story many times in my work with couples that one or the other or both knew on the way to the altar that it was a mistake. Something caused them to override their instincts and they proceeded smiling. Their instincts and intuition had been shut down or, if they did feel uneasy, they thought that they were in too deep…what would people think if they changed their minds?

The common experience for many people whom I have seen and also for myself is the lack of parental guidance. Thus, we become prey to the energy that seduces us into doing the very thing we **instinctively** feared or we had reservations about, or could feel in our bones.

There is little understanding of what is covert within – a smooth operator. Many clients have reported confusing and difficult situations that they have experienced because of knowing instinctively yet, somehow they were convinced by some force within that it was alright to proceed especially if some pleasures of the ego were involved. They have assured themselves that "it will be alright" and close the door on their own truths.

It is natural for all of us to want everything to be wonderful but, this is an adolescent desire for paradise here on earth. This idea, along with naivete, sets us up for the inner predator to take over (an inner coup d'etat!)…the element of surprise…when you least expect it…when you're unprepared for it…even the warning signs. There are false promises based on contrivances such as "it is for your own good" which conjure up the dark Bin Laden energy within.

Women especially are taught at a very early age through the socialization process, to override their instincts in order to adapt and "make nice" all manner of atrocities. In other words, not to see what they see or to feel what they feel. The meta-message is that having perception and vision is dangerous to the status quo. "Keep quiet" becomes the inner and outer mandate. In other words, girls are trained in submissiveness and are ripe for capture in the inner world as well as the outer world.

Tied-Up

When did it start
this knot around her heart
this corded constriction?
What convoluted matrix
led to this twisted conformity?
Early abnegation and violation?
Later penetration and dismissal?
The spear-like pains reach climax
Replete from spasm she
grabs and grasps for breath
The downward spiral threatens
She's there! Face to face
with the haunting loneliness
that has threatened since long ago
The grey cloud masked a black shroud
which impeded vision and left her
immobile and negated

The truth is that we need a couple of things. One, is a proper attitude towards consciousness. Two, is that we need to honour the impulse to uncover facts. This is what I am trying to do in this work.

Make no mistake; our fundamental power is **natural curiosity**. Those tics and nudges we feel at times have much to teach us if only we would listen to and pay attention to them! If only we would not get entangled with the Bin Laden psychic force which is against what is natural to us. This is what prevents us from knowing what we really do know down and deep.

Freedom

What is that?
I know "knot"
Having been so tied
Up or is it down?
I know "knot"
In this time of dread
the closet opens
no more illusions
All is bared or
is it barred?
Only that I have seen
and can feel no more
Can't even try
No breath no fire
flat weary
finished
I know!

IT'S NOT THE ANSWERS-
IT'S THE QUESTIONS

We must all learn to formulate the questions that probe and help us to peer beyond the veils of illusion. I know this to be true from my career as a therapist. I work on the questions in order to draw the clients into an alliance with me against their dark man within. I know that the questions come from the curiosity about what lies behind what is being presented as if in one's best interests in the moment. I am talking about moment to moment awareness and being able to stay on top of the predatory energies that stalk and stop our development.

In other words, I ask them to summon up the predator so we can focus our gaze and **not** dissociate. This is not an easy task. It brings up a great deal of fear and anxiety. I help people to name their feelings that naturally come up with any change in one's perspective. Eventually, of course, behavioural change follows. I encourage them as they do in AA programs to "fake it until you make it"; in other words, to act according to what they are learning or bringing to the light of consciousness. This is like systematic desensitization which, over time, shifts the framework of their thoughts. Their behaviour becomes more congruent with their increasing confidence in themselves. This is about finishing the individuation imperative so that they can fly from the nest into the world.

A New Day

It is a spring day
The pond is still
No ripples to be seen
Mother and father goose
stay close as ten little
goslings play at their feet

The babies will not go
into the water without
their mother who guards

them cautiously
attended by the father
on alert to any
present danger

She slides into the water
gliding smoothly guiding
her loved ones into
nature's moist place where
they bob and dive in glee
under fond embrace

Mother leads, they follow
Father pulls up the rear
protecting his exquisite brood
They all negotiate the embankment
with such skill
There is no hesitation in their movement
up the incline to known safety.

I stand and watch with wonder
The moisture is now in the eyes
of a woman with unresolved grief
over past losses and with new fears
of high banks and threatening waters.

In the process of uncovering, I become a counter magician. Asking the proper questions is the key to catching the dark image with his "pants down". This Bin Laden energy is being exposed and the secret cave where he lurks begins to appear.

Through a process of dialogue, drawing pictures and images of the dark side, having people do corresponding movements depicting these images and encouraging writing about these images, I bear high witness to their confrontation with the "death-bringer". This is what negative energy does. It saps life. It drains and can bring death. The writing, particularly, helps to ground the free-floating anxiety that bubbles up. After all, they have their Bin Laden "stuff" staring them right in the face…it is frightening to face what defeating energies one has buried.

This is a process which brings maturity to the formerly naive as they venture to look what is in front of them or behind their "front". We peer at a secret something, a forbidden something that has been sucking them dry. Many people have been physically sick from it, or have no energy, or are down and depressed. They often wonder what is the point of it all. They are too weary to keep up their façade, their mask, their "front".

Unmasked, these people are looking at their dark demon (s). Face to face! What would you do if suddenly Bin Laden appeared in front of you? At this point, these people are tapping into their inner wisdom. The substance of the matter is laid open to them. This is **vital vision.**

Courage

It takes the strong knight
to fight – to grow
as slow as it may seem
the scabbard
forces order in a criminal world
where some flee in fear
when old burdens portend
and cowards
fend with lies

THE INNER ASSASSIN-

RETRIEVAL

Just as we were shocked by the carnage in New York City on September 11, 2001, so too can we be shocked by the carnage in some part of our deeper selves. Both are real. We **know** something is wrong. We may try to hide from the devastation in our personal lives by pretending everything is fine but the loss of energy or rage will continue until we recognize the dark magician, the Bin Laden energy, for what it truly is.

When we can peer into our own lives and witness carnage, lost opportunities, dashed hopes and dreams and so on, we often find that there has been an inner assassin cutting us off from life's flow. We discover lifeless thoughts, feelings and desires. We have been kept very busy but it hasn't gotten us anywhere. We have truly been lost in the Land of Oz and the dark wizard is really a sham!

The emphasis on the failure of the intelligence operations in the U.S. and much of the world, I believe, has more to do with lack of wisdom not intelligence. Perhaps it is about the unconscious unwillingness to look behind so very many of the illusions contained in the American Dream ideology with its empty "paradisical" promises. In other words, we don't even know that we don't want to look and see. Perhaps it is as simple as the "powers that be" showing their dark side by manipulating the information to satisfy their ulterior motives. That the United States of America is still in its' adolescence is underscored by its ambivalence in Afghanistan. (All adolescents are somewhat "borderline" in their ambivalence about wanting to stay or to leave what they believe is their secure base with their parents and their ideologies before they wander and explore new terrain which will bring them to powerful inner security over time).

The U.S. feeds at one end and takes at the other. You can not burn the candle at both ends. The emphasis on materialism and capitalism is no longer serving citizens who are searching for some union that seems so elusive. We are all scarred and scared. Perhaps we could change the letter "c" in both words and emphasize the **sacred**. We can no longer tolerate malevolence disguised as benevolence.

Buried Alive

I'll light a candle for you
Is that all you can say
after all mother fucker?
Light a candle gentle coward?
Is that all you can say
to a woman who would soothe amuse
so you could abuse and disregard her
in one foul swoop of your
narcissistic commentary?
Who are you anyway?

Master Magician writer pimp
therapist priest outcast dumper
secret thumper?
I've had enough of your blunder
your thunder your saccharin
lies and pretense
Get out! Get out! Get out!

Listen to my heart's song

EARLY WARNING SYSTEM-
THE KILLING FIELD

When one carries naive presentments about someone or something, or avoids the truth of one's own devastation, there most certainly will be warnings. Will we see the signs or listen in time? These warnings that show up in dreams, nightmares and illnesses often go unheeded yet, they are the precursors of opportunity for more expansive living and spiritual development.

When our lives seem incongruent with our inner desires, there are spores around which have been left and are proof of the dark mage, Bin Laden. When we give up after the first hardship; when we procrastinate or find countless reasons to sabotage our desires, the dark magician is at work creating self-hatred, shame, blame and guilt. This predatory energy is always trying to derail us. It wants to get us off course in terms of self-development and self-actualization with its, "Oh, I can't because I don't have enough money, my father needs me, my kids are too young, I'm too old, what would people think?".

We must begin to see the truth of it all, to be adequately perceptive, to hold our perceptions, truths and instincts in consciousness and to **take action** which will lead to resolution.

When my clients arrive at the point where they see the decimation of the deepest and most soulful aspects of their creative lives, the rage surfaces. This is the energy that was behind the near perfect personas or "fronts" or facades. This is the "crying time" and they can no longer hide their anger and sorrow. I know because I have been there.

These men and women find themselves in this process, in the killing field of the psychic predator and no longer can they pretend it doesn't exist. This process is very painful. It is about **conscious** suffering, a far cry from martyrdom and disenfranchisement. They are coming to life through the valley of tears. It is so horrible and so sick that they cry.

Desperation

The killing room calls
I will not succumb
Bent from relapse
I marry faith
and see tomorrow

The pen gives paint
to a shadow piqued
by life's rough edge
I stand poised
to greet the sun

When we can face the truth of what has gone on for far too long, we are truly at the point of developing new and interesting aspects of the self. We are deepening our capacity for compassion, connection, insight, inspiration, right action and so forth. No longer will we be content to live marginal lives, duped by false promises and emphasis on national security and ego.

The disarming questions must be asked just as they are in therapeutic process. When we begin to shine the light on our own darkness, we find darker and even darker areas. The questions **must** be answered. It follows that the deepest inner work is the darkest. We must be brave and unafraid, (just as it was asked of us after September 11th), to investigate the worst in order to increase personal and spiritual power.

We continue to grow when we continue to wake up to the truth of our unlived lives. We can enter into the process of soul making and, in so doing, bring ourselves back to life. There is no question that we can break old patterns of ignorance. We have witnessed horror and we can not back away. We must take a stand. This is indeed the right time to take action – banishing, transforming or exterminating the predator.

THE KILLING FORCE

This is the Crucifixion: which can lead to ascension. Clients do not hear me at this point. Seeing and feeling the truth takes them more deeply into the depression or rage. They descend into a place where they feel raw, naked and vulnerable. It is like a lobster shedding its skin. They go to a safe place to do it because they know they're going to be raw and vulnerable for awhile until their shell gets harder. These clients are not sure at all about this consciousness they bravely seek. Even Christ asked his father to relieve him of this anguish; "Father let this cup pass from me".

The killing force, the Bin Laden, will continue to check in and try again to get one off track from time to time, even after the client has done this hard work. The dark image will dig in its heels even harder in order to arrest new growth and development. It is in its nature to seduce and defy. (One more time, maybe I'll get her this time; maybe he's weakened by now)... We have to be vigilant in our quest to become whole, not perfect, in this lifetime.

Ambivalence

Uneasiness brings reprimand
An internal appeal for favour
challenges an ambivalence
so ornery it shapes dread
and digs up fear
New bargains bring regret
and relief is relative
to a faith in bones and
retrieval of old orders
once negated and dismissed
A tiredness weakens resolve
as negative refrain takes refuge
in training and odd favour
The slide reveals substance
in the shaky lament

FORGET THE PAST: GET ON WITH LIFE

At this difficult time in therapy, as well as in our history, we all want to forget we witnessed the carnage. It is natural to want to censor all negative and painful events. We will attempt everything we know to try to end the process by pretending it isn't occurring or that it has ever occurred.

This is a time of accepting death. Dying to the old life is required. Things will never be the same. We are being awakened personally and collectively through the loss of vital life as in the real losses on September 11th and November 12th as well as the loss of vital life force in so many men and women who are depressed, angry and sad. Perhaps it is a time to begin to really live.

If we continue to ignore and to not investigate our own issues and places of deadness and murder, personally and collectively, we will remain obedient to the Bin Laden energy. Only if we make this effort will we finally see behind the façade of wealth, false power and security. We stand on the threshold of being able to see how captured we really are and how much of our God-given vital life is "at the stake". **We can do something even more powerful.**

Finished

Never again will I wear
the mask
that covered the lies
That gave order to that
onerous task of uncovering

A / THE HOLY WAR–

(SOVEREIGNTY)

We can gain sovereignty over our own lives only when we can outwit and outsmart the predatory murderous element of our unconscious, on both a personal and collective level. It has been asked, "what do women want?". The answer is, "we want sovereignty over our own lives" – meaning, of course, power to control our own lives and be the authors of our individual destinies. Men need this as well.

We can attack from the rear or just dive right into the issue and see it from an entirely different perspective. It is at this point that we become cunning. We stall for time. We strengthen during this period and we bide our time planning strategy and summoning power from within ourselves. At the same time, mark my words, the predator will threaten by taking this as a challenge.

This is the boiling point. This is the time to kill this dark, inhibiting energy force, when it is becoming more murderous. It is though he has smelled blood and it makes him crazy. It is now a true holy war and a holy "making". It must be driven out because of the depth of its evil...and it is getting worse now that we have activated a response. Under the pressure of the assassin, a weariness may set in, inhibiting our resolve. We must muster all our resources in order to keep moving forward. We must not go to sleep which could bring certain death. We must stay conscious and awake to the truth of the dark mage's devastation.

It is at this point of discovery that we can move from victim status to the status of shrewd warrior. Continuing to stay curious and to formulate key questions help even as the predator continues to plan our death – (the death of our spirit most definitely, but in many cases it is also the death of our dreams, the ability to imagine and care, and eventually actual death often results). This is now a psychic dance. It is crucial that we not become afraid or grovel. This is the time for solid grounding and all-out war against this atrocious murderer within. It is only then that we will be able to stop **projecting outwardly** which creates Hitlers and Bin Ladens. No one can carry this kind of energy without going mad. (Remember what they said about Hitler at the end?…crazed, demonic).

Heathcliff

What of this fascination
compelling and dangerous
at the same time
I was drawn to it
a long time ago
when I was bound
by invisible chains
and protective armour
being woman yet aware
of that Darkness
that alter ego so
indefinable at the time
The gnawing in my soul
would not hold out
for safety in conformity
It drove me to formulate the question
and to begin the Affair with myself
Maiden fair and dark shadow
"Who am I?" said she
"Let me lead" said he
A twist of fate
began the dance
man - woman woman – man
shadow prince and maiden fair

AGENTIC IN OUR OWN LIVES-
VICTIM NO MORE

We all have to work hard now, at this point in our lives and in our world, to rouse the energy required to overwhelm the captor both in our psyche and in our outer world, be it religion, family, culture, husband, wife, child or friend. This is a time for an intra-psychic power-surge.

It is a time for the wise feminine energies to summon up healthy masculine ones which are trained to fight to the death. These healthy masculine energies are about responsible stewardship. These aspects of the psyche are not always available so we have to focus and summon them up. (Remember President George W. Bush's words that he was "extremely focused"). The fighting nature within is fierce and contentious. It will defend until the end to retrieve vital life. In my opinion, vital life is a God-given birthright and, thus, is a morally justifiable war.

The wonderful thing is that the integration of wise feminine and healthy masculine energies provide a united front line defense. As the internal feminine wisdom is strengthening, the internal masculine energy will rally to her cause and will assist in her bid for consciousness. (As it is "out there", it is "in here"). Internal thought and feeling now become **connected** in the inner world and signal the time to implement ideas. This is the blessing of the blending of strength and action.

This is the template for healing as I see it. It is my truth and I dare you to discover your personal truth. You **can** change your world and, in so doing, you affect your entire galaxy. It begins with **you**.

May the force be with you.
You are the most important component in the future of the world.

Medicine Woman

I am your medicine
What is it in you
that defends against
such wholeness?
Is the bad taste
more about physical
sensation than disgrace?

Move away Lord
of the temple
give room to the
bedrock of desire
Magdalene was not
interested in His loins

She needed the
Lord of the Dance
Why won't you
dance with me?

WHAT IF WE...........?

- could find rooms for men and women to gather together and work towards greater consciousness....
- could find a safe place to share....
- could have discourse without debate....
- could write in stream of consciousness with no censor....
- could draw the images that we naturally think in and move them out....
- could honour sanity and softer skill....
- could encourage right action....
- could experience our imminent spirits so as to feel a greater attunement to all that is....
- could come together in ritual that connects us to the sacred....
- could dance our dreams...
- could move out the murderous internal energies....
- could sing and open our hearts....
- could develop compassion, to negotiate and to get language for what we feel...for our emotional lives.

What **would** our world be like........?

PART II

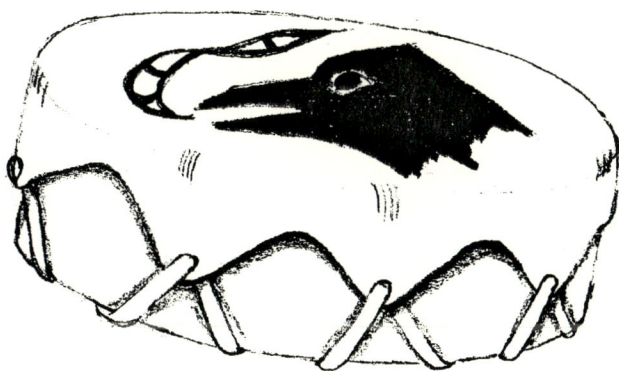

NOW SADDAM HUSSEIN ... WHO/WHAT IS NEXT?

I ask as I sit here a year and a half after September 11th 2001 : "Have we cried the tears that matter?" In my opinion, the United States politicians have only found excuses for further violence which may be winding its way to the finish line as we stand on the brink of nuclear warfare. Is this what it will take to make us wake up to the dark side of absolute power that has corrupted absolutely? I am truly afraid that we will not wake up in time as we know it.

We have people in power who are incapable of formulating important questions but who are quick to have the answers in concrete, rationalistic and absolutistic thought forms.

What about the question of why are we here? We have been given the gift of life and what are most of us doing with the privilege of being on this beautiful, fragile planet?

The greatest diseases of our time are greed and addiction. The emphasis has been on accumulation and consumption on a runaway mode. We have created a world that is out of control and we are finding ourselves estranged from the organic pattern of life that is embedded in our neurons and the universe itself. We are all one people when it comes down to basic truth but find ourselves estranged from the self, the other, the Earth and the Creator.

We have madmen trying to play the authoritarian "God the Father" and followers in an unconscious, somnambulistic state ready to jump to their every word. Hitler's SS men were mainly Roman Catholic soldiers who were waiting for a demi-god to follow due to personal emptiness. It may seem easier to live with an exterior God or authority than to recognize the need for self responsibility and self cultivation. I am speaking now in terms of required individuation that is a process of extending the boundaries of awareness and of expanding the boundaries of our personalities. This is about growing up.

I am proud that Canada has taken a stand against involvement in the War on Iraq. She is growing up and out. She is dissenting which is healthy and no longer blindly obedient to Great Britain and its Imperialism or to The United States and its emphasis on Nationalism and heroics.
Canada has taken a humanitarian stance and is formulating important questions and it is time.

To hide from this accountability, humanity has created or developed innumerable scapegoats and escape routes. Exteriorized religious practices make scapegoats of minority groups, women, children or other individuals. Rigid beliefs in a political system or philosophy, a search for "samadhi", or god, or as a final solution, suicide, are but escape routes from personal and collective responsibility. Canada is becoming more skeptical as all of us should and in that process find a deeper sense of self in our connection with the cosmos. In this way, we can move out of addiction to power and control. What if each of us knew that we are the God, or the divinity, that we search for and could recognize that in each other? Would we be so apt to murder, terrorize and corrupt just to prove the point of our worthiness or entitlement?

We all leave the world naked except for the inner quality of our being. I believe that our purpose here on this "earthwalk" is to cultivate just that, no matter what race or colour. This meeting of the self in all its deep feeling of connection, its uncertainty, its vulnerability is not without pain and joy. It means that, at times, we have to turn the spotlight on the gloom that surrounds us and continue to trust in a process that is constantly reflected in the cycles of nature. Core issues come up over and over again for healing at higher levels of development each time. This is how we continue to expand our consciousness and there can be so much joy and awe in the 'knowing down and deep".

Canada is at the threshold now. Will she be able to hold the tension between the opposites of what is deemed right or wrong and hold her place as a great country of the world who has chosen to map new territory? She is curious, dissenting and waking up to herself.

May she stand for truth, wisdom, discernment and responsibility.

HO! CANADA!

AND THE BEAT GOES ON...AND ON...AND ON...AND ON

It has been two years to the day since the September 11th massacre and one year since I completed the first section of this book. I felt mired at many levels; my own predator had me second guessing as to the merits of my work; the presses to which I submitted my manuscript said they wouldn't touch anything that had to do with September 11th; I was dealing with many external pressures that sapped my energy, physically, emotionally and spiritually. I remember once being told that, when one feels stuck, the most important question to formulate is, "Who needs my help now?"

The emphasis was not on self-sacrifice or martyrdom but rather on the notion that moving from a loving heart to help another, or others, would result in a stripping away of any layers of self-doubt and then doubt by others would gradually slip away. This is exactly the position I am now in; one of strength, conviction and a desire for truth. I began to write again as I witnessed a world being torn apart by arrogance, greed, ego and emphasis on national security. I wanted to help.

I remember my grandmother telling me a tale when I was pre-school age. She told me that it was a story for those who were not faint of heart. She must have sensed spiritual strength in me and I now recognize that, if it wasn't for my faith and strength, I would not be sitting here writing. I may have died, succumbed to addiction to more destructive opiates than depression or have been killed off in one way or another. What I knew, what I said, what I represented at some level or another has been deemed dangerous, I know! It has taken act upon act drenched in courage to stay "alive".

The fairy tale I am about to share with you concerns shadow. Shadow is a dark truth that sits close to the surface of our conscious mind in the subconscious. It is protected from making itself known through denial systems that are centuries old and have to do with the entrenchment of "power over" and rigid systems of control, both political and religious. Presented as if "in everyone's best interest", these systems have murderous intentions at their core. What has been killed off is respect for feminine instinct, intuition and wisdom.

I am not being gender specific but refer rather to energies that are within both men and women. These energies have been "put asunder" for the purpose of maintaining status quo and emphasis on gross national product. If we could really appreciate the natural world and the natural order of things, we would know "in our bones" that change is the only poem and our purpose on this earth-walk is to come to greater awareness of our "at-one-ment". We must not succumb to the pernicious influence of patriarchal power structures and emphasize atonement and more joy in heaven. This paradigm promotes the martyrdom and disenfranchisement that leads to the violence in the world that has become the "whore of the powerless".

Goodbye Kate

What is your passion
Black-haired floozy?
You dance
a murderous dance
into crescendo
What was the set-up
crippled waif?
Twirled and gagged
by tight disorder
the past paints present
with liquid hate
How can I help you
woman/child?
There is no glint
in that vacuous glare
You clutch and you cringe
dancing out of control
Goodbye Kate
a murdered soul

GRANDMA'S TALE

I could have looked up the original tale of Bluebeard but I wanted to share with you the way that it was told to me. In my respect for the oral traditions where stories were handed down by word of mouth from generation to generation, I will relate a mystery laid out for me by an older woman of wisdom. This was a woman who possessed a deep knowing without the language that I would come to "know" after a life of "lived" experiences in a world gone mad with power. This woman was my grandmother.

"Fear not little one as I weave this tale, for there is much to learn and to know", she would begin.

There was a shank of beard that was kept by nuns in the far mountains. No one seemed to know how it came to be in their possession but the only ones to ever touch it were these mothers who seemed to be unaffected by it. It is said that the beard was as blue as the hole of a shadow at night and that it was once worn by a man who was a failed magician and womanizer.
He was a man known as Bluebeard.

Legend says that he attempted to court three sisters at once. They were all frightened of his beard so they hid whenever he came to call on them. He was intent on convincing the sisters of his good intentions so he asked them to picnic with him in the forest. He arrived decked out in finery leading horses sporting bells and red ribbons. He invited their mother to accompany them and set them all in his horse cart ready for a fine day. They had a most wonderful time riding and, when they stopped, he fed them sweets and told them stories. He did such a good job in fact, that the mother and sisters began to think that he was not so bad after all in spite of his horrible beard.

They returned home excited and full of chatter trying to convince one another that it had been a delightful and interesting time. Yet, the two eldest sisters felt suspicious and, in spite of obvious pleasure, they vowed never to see Bluebeard again. The youngest sister, however, was swayed by his charms and thought they were being ridiculous. The more she talked to them and to herself, the less hideous he seemed.

When Bluebeard asked her to marry him, she accepted. She gave his proposal great thought and felt that she had found her prince. They were married and rode off to his castle in the woods.

One day, he came to tell her that he was going away for a time and suggested that she invite her family over. He gave her permission to use the kitchen and arrange a dinner party. He left her a ring of keys telling her to open any door in the castle, including the money rooms, but that she was not to use the key with the scrollwork on top. Bluebeard's wife complied and said that she would do all that he asked and bade her husband good-bye. Off he rode into the forest and she busied herself with arrangements for the party.

Her sisters arrived at the castle and, as they had always been of the curious sort, they asked their sister about his wishes while he was away. The young wife told them. "He said that we could enter any room we wish except one. I do not know which one it is, only that I have a key and no idea which door it fits".

The sisters decided to make a game out of finding the forbidden door. The castle was three stories high and had hundreds of doors and there were as many keys on the ring. They were so excited going from door to door finding the kitchen stores, the money rooms and many, many things that seemed so wonderful with each opening. After a long time, and, having seen so many marvels, they came to the cellar. At the end of the corridor was a blank wall. They were puzzled over the tiny key with the scrollwork that didn't fit any door so far. Just as they recognized this, they saw a small door about to close. When they tried to open it again, it was securely locked. One sister cried out to the youngest to bring the key. Immediately, one of the sisters put the key into the lock and slowly turned it. The lock clicked and the door swung open but the room was so dark that they couldn't see. They found a candle and lit it. They held it into the room and all three began screaming. The room was full of blood and black bones of corpses that were strewn about. Numerous skulls were stacked in the corners.

They slammed the door and shook the key out of the lock as they breathlessly hugged one another. "Oh my god, my god!", they exclaimed. The wife looked down at the key that was now stained with blood and hurriedly tried to wipe it clean with her skirt. The key kept bleeding as each sister took her turn at wiping it. The blood remained.

At this point in the story, my Granny would check to see that I was awake and that I could tolerate hearing more.

"Oh, yes Granny! I want to hear more. I wonder what Bluebeard will do when he finds out?", I replied.

"Okay, darling", she would say. "But put your hand in mine so I can ground you". I did not know then what grounding meant but I gave her my hand and felt her pulse beating time with mine. We became one in the flesh.

The wife hid the tiny key in her pocket and ran to the cook in the kitchen to fetch some horsehair. Her dress was stained and the key was still oozing dark red blood. Even the horsehair didn't help. She went outside and pressed ashes from the fire into her dress, scrubbing it more. She held the key to the heat to scorch it and laid cobwebs over it to stem the flow but nothing worked.

"What am I going to do", she cried and threw her dress into the wardrobe and closed the door. "It is all a bad dream", she told herself. "It will be alright…I know it will", she lied.

Bluebeard returned home the next morning and immediately looked for his wife.

"Well, how was it while I was away?", he asked.

"It was lovely sir", the young wife answered.

"How are my storage rooms?"

"Fine, sir…very fine".

"How are my money rooms?"

"Fine, sir, everything is fine".

"Well, you'd best return my keys then!"

Within seconds, Bluebeard realized that the small key was missing and he seized his wife by the hair.

"You traitor!", he snarled and threw her to the floor. "You've been into the room, have you not?!"

With that statement, he flung open her wardrobe and the little key that was on the top shelf had bled its red down all of her beautiful gowns that were hanging there.

"Now it's your turn girlie!", he screamed and dragged her down into the cellar until they were in front of that terrible door. Bluebeard had only to look at the door with his fiery eyes and it opened. There lay the skeletons of all his former wives. His wife caught hold of the door frame and wouldn't let go as he roared, "It's time for you!". She begged him to grant her some time to compose herself and prepare for her death. She asked for just fifteen minutes before he took her life so that she could make her peace with God.

"All right. You can have but a quarter of an hour, but be ready", he snarled.

His wife ran up the stairs to her bedroom and told her sisters to wait on the castle ramparts. She knelt as if to pray but called out instead to her sisters.

"Sisters, sisters, do you see the brothers coming?"

"We see nothing ahead", they answered.

Every few minutes she cried up at the ramparts, "Sisters, sisters. Do you see the brothers coming yet?"

"We see a whirlwind, perhaps a dust devil in the distance".

Meanwhile, Bluebeard roared for her to return to the cellar to face her beheading. Again she cried out, "Sisters, sisters, do you see our brothers coming?"

Bluebeard shouted for her again and began to clomp up the stairs to her bedroom. Her sisters cried out, "Yes, we see them! Our brothers have come and they have just entered the castle!"

Bluebeard yelled, "I am coming to get you!" His footsteps were so heavy that some of the rocks in the hallway came loose from the mortar that held them. As Bluebeard moved towards his wife with his hands outstretched to seize her, the brothers entered the castle hallway and rode into her room on horseback. There, they forced Bluebeard onto the parapet and, with swords drawn, they moved towards him striking, slashing, cutting, whipping and beating the predator to the ground. They killed him at last and left his blood, bones and tissue for the scavengers.

At the end of the story, my Granny would tuck me in and tell me that I did not have to worry about Bluebeard if I recited after her, "Dear God, I ask that you send all negative energy to the light to be transformed". I always did as she said and then she would sing "An Irish Lullaby" to me. I always heard the end of the song but went to sleep soundly knowing that I was safe with her and at one with the people of the world.

I now suspect that she was trying to tell me something that she knew deep down in her heart and flesh that neither of us had language for. I would someday find the language, however, after a delayed childhood when one is kept naïve; groomed and schooled in the precepts and invectives of a culture that would keep me stuck in concrete thought. My religion underscored those strictures by using "escatalogical" scares about heaven and hell to prevent doubt or curiosity. I was mandated at every level to act like a good woman and to think like a child. Abstract thought could be very dangerous in the scheme of things so I learned to keep a tight hold on the night; or should I say, keep a lid on what I knew deep inside of me. And now…I have become dissident and able to formulate questions and "flesh out" answers. I invite you to "look" with me – to peer into the truth.

The concept of "fleshing out" a tale has to do with reverence for the feminine ability to be creative in that one is able to access an inner voice that allows one to find different ways of saying, or seeing, the same thing. Psychoanalysts use the term "stream of consciousness" to describe just that. It is about allowing for a free flow of ideas as a way around inner censorship that stifles growth and overrides intuition.

If one were to "flesh out" Bluebeard for example, one might get: dark as you can get; strange colour; night time blue; etc. I will go on as an invitation to you to do the same with all that comes to you as standard or "pat" answers.

Bluebeard is courting three sisters and a mother as the story begins. If one "fleshed" courting, one might come up with: coming to call; putting the best foot forward; overcoming resistance; enticing; hiding; shadow; sugar coating; tricking; playing up to; appealing to; finding the soft spot; or perhaps, "working the room".

We face American dominance in the 21st century with its invincible military and claims to having the guts to use it. I believe it is important to "flesh out" the doctrine of the American regime's New World Order that is meant to charm and seduce as Bluebeard did in his campaign to entice the sisters who had a naïve mother who colludes into his territory.

I ask you – War? How are we being seduced?

I invite you now to "flesh" my grandmother's tale with me as we peer into things and nose out some facts about what has truly gone on in the name of progress.

Notice what happens to the older sisters in the story. You will see that they use their thoughts to support their instincts. The youngest sister is too identified with naivete and shuts down; or should I say, that she cannot access her innate instincts and feminine wisdom just like her mother. The older sisters have a knowing which warns against romancing the predator, Bluebeard. They sense the credibility gap very soon between what he says to them at the picnic and what he does.

I ask you now; what voices in your psyche do you continue to ignore that warn you away from danger and manipulation? Remember throughout this investigation that I present that the political becomes the personal. What happens at the collective level goes on in our personal psyches and serves to maintain the status quo, our illusions and delusions.

The shrewd attacker, Bluebeard, senses who is willing prey and goes after the youngest sister. She is naïve, inexperienced, uninformed and foolish. This mage who has enough knowledge of human behaviour in order to manipulate, tries to create an extraordinary experience. When in your life have you had suspicions and fears? How did you deal with them? How have you talked your way out of situations that portended trouble? How are we trained to overcome the energies of suspicion and fear? Who benefits from this reflex?

Notice that, as the young sister talks to herself, her vision changes…"she thought she was about to marry a very elegant man". She persuades herself that he is not dangerous but rather eccentric and idiosyncratic. It is true that, when our alarm systems are not well developed, we get charmed when we are told, especially, that what is being done is in our best interests. We get captivated as a result of denying our instincts. Often, the spin doctors formulate stories or manipulate the facts to suit their own, or their leaders' selfish interests or personal bias.

In a moment of youthful exuberance, of folly, pleasure and intrigue, the young sister is swayed as to the predator's beneficence. Is this what the emphasis on nationhood does to most of us, especially the young men and women who put their lives on the line in wars that do not make much sense? Is this why the prayer of allegiance is recited every school day because the conceptual ability of the young is concrete? Their tendency is to take everything literally until someone with wisdom comes along to encourage them to think in the abstract and to individuate from what they believed was security and to find their own. If parents are trained to bind their children to them through thorough training in the invectives of a culture that seems to promise security, then they will create the same. The same is not always healthy or relevant to the time. Isn't this what "party politics" is all about? Witness this in the present political situation where, simply because prior generations have voted along one party line, the successive generations are expected to follow suit. Remember that the mother was naïve in the story and that no father seemed to be present.

Materna Introjecta

Where are you mom?
What is behind the haze
in your once so bright hazel eyes?

What dreams went underground
when you began the life
of submission
to wills cemented through pain?

I need you mom – just for
some blessing because life has
become very difficult
and I find myself succumbing
to the seduction of that constriction
so embedded in our womanly psyches

The lashes smart
my body cries out for comfort
Is there anyone home?
Where are you mom?

I am reminded of the story of Adam and Eve that has been used so often to keep women, especially, in their place. What is this place? I believe it is about the promise of a paradise if one does not ask questions. The God that most of us have been trained to worship in Christian Patriarchy is the punishing one who banishes the man and woman that he created for asking questions. Who had the most courage in the story? I say it was Eve who had outgrown the world of animal existence and had the courage to enter the world of complicated moral expectations. She is the one who is the most brave. She is not easily seduced, frivolous or disobedient. Perhaps most of us have bought into a distorted story that has been misinterpreted in order to paint her as villain and responsible for all of the world's problems. She was giving us humanity with all of its pain and all of its richness. She gave us a bigger life than mere dependency on the will and benevolence of the gods who just might have been withholding the good things. She only wanted to graduate beyond mere animal existence and knew that there must be more to life than eating and mating. She wanted Adam to share in that life and he seemed willing to take the chance. They had to face the fact that there was Good and Evil in a world where they would make many mistakes, not because they were weak or bad, but because the choices they would have to make would be difficult ones. The satisfactions, however, were equally great because, while animals can only be useful and obedient, human beings can be good. This I see as a story of the emergence of humankind and one of the most liberating events in the history of mankind.

The consequences were painful but anyone who has experienced the complex and hard-earned satisfactions of human existence would have to say that it was worth the pain. This is the pain that brings us all more fully alive. We have to face growing pains as we move beyond the dependency solutions of childhood and wrestle with the ambivalence of staying safe with what is known and what might be. We have to develop courage and understand what being a healthy warrior is about as we take on the task of moving beyond the development of those who went before us. Only then can we come to a mature vision of the world and our place in it. This is what would bring one back to the garden; that "Edenic" experience that we long for as manifested in our addictions, especially to "power over". We can find that place only when we can arrive at seeing all of creation with the eyes of a child and enjoy life through the accumulated wisdom of life's experiences. This is certainly not about atonement and fear of punishment for having authentic curiosity and farsightedness.

The Summons

Thou art a fierce God
whom I tremble to confront
This soul is once again in the hour of darkness
frightened, confused and frustrated
fresh from those experiences
where passivity and diminishment
ruptured happiness
Can the spell be broken?

The kingdom be renewed?
It is within as it is without
Do I dare? Once again…the question
There was no wisdom in Bluebeard
What of this Beast
who sets the challenge?
I cannot dissolve…escape or deny now
Redemption is in me…I am prisoner
before I become master once again
This fearful task beckons me to
embrace a power nontransferable
I am that monster…that Beast
You are in me as I am in you
We are one and I have come to love you

I ask you now: What other ways are there of saying "obey me?" If I "flesh out" I might say: Ask no questions; Do as I say; How dare you question my motives, I have your best interests at heart. What might you add to this list? What is our culture and our leaders asking from us at this difficult time in our history? Witness political addresses where the rhetoric and mannerisms used are carefully choreographed to instill quiet in those who do not subscribe to these opinions (i.e. un-American) does this also mean that the entire populace should follow one party's New Order" simply because it's expected and, therefore, patriotic of them to do so even if they don't believe in it? To take this one step further, are all other countries in the world expected to abide by another country's dictates as well or suffer the consequences?

Let us take a look at the set-up in the story of Bluebeard. The younger sister agrees to marry a force that she believes to be very elegant based on his appearances and promises of a better life. So many of us are vulnerable to seeing only the overt presentation. Not only is the youngest naïve about her own mental processes, but also about the murdering aspect of her own psyche that lures her through the promise of pleasure for the ego. We do, all of us, have a yen for the "paradisaical" which keeps us in perpetual adolescence. This desire, combined with naivete, makes us food for the predator inside as well as outside of us all.

This malignant force is in opposition to what is natural to us in terms of intuition and instinct. We are, I believe, a culture of "instinct wounded" individuals who operate in a collective that has grown to love the drug dealer of psychic highs manifesting through rampant addiction to "power over", war, relationships, sex and drugs. It is the promise of ease that seduces us. Like Eve, we must recognize the dark aspects of this promise and protect ourselves from the devastation. We must ultimately deprive this trickster of its murderous energy. We must grow up and mature so as not to become vulnerable out of naivete, foolishness, inexperience or fear. In the current political climate, has Canada not reached this point by taking a firm stand and refusing to go into a conflict alongside our neighbours to the south? In the past, Canada and other nations have entered into agreements that were touted to be beneficial to all participants. Through experience, we now know that the country that proposes these agreements is usually the one that benefits the most. It is also the aggressor at generating things such as excessive trade tariffs or embargoes as soon as it feels that any of its business is being compromised.

Defeated

She couldn't get to town
they wouldn't let her
those who knew to fake
and lie and help themselves to power
Will she get her bearings
on that sea of tomorrows
bent from relapse
her spine giving way
to pretense?

How have you been trained to override your intuition?

In the tale, the natural response of the sisters to Bluebeard's mandate, "Do not use this key!", is to stay curious. This is the only way, I believe, that we can hold on to what is most vital in us. It is the way to maintain the creative and pure vision of a child fresh from the Creator and one not sullied from constantly being told that, "This is for your own good!", which has often been very disparate from one's experienced reality.

Notice that the bride is compliant. What Bluebeard does not want from his wife is freedom, knowledge and personal power. This young woman has been forced into believing that she is powerless and it is true. She has been captured right at the time of her unfolding or blossoming and has already begun to comply with the promise that she will become a queen while her murder is being planned from the start. Is this what keeps happening to our young men and women who are enticed into combat and the support of war? What false promises lure them into situations that take their vital lives both literally and figuratively? Is this not the face of Evil? Whether it is intentional or not is not the issue. What is the bad deal is that these young people are vulnerable to promises made by leaders that it is in the troops' best interest to defend their nation while those in power sit protected by their illusions and high security which keeps the delusions alive. This is treachery of the highest order and I ask you: What is the true agenda here? Are they being used and abused by those in power to perpetuate their intent to create a world order that, in reality, is no different than that which the deluded mad man, Adolf Hitler, envisioned?

Fed-up

*This is but lip service
A display that cannot fool
one who has known but
has learned to be quiet
in service*

*Is it only for you?
I have come to hate you
for such pretense and vague truths
that mask dark powers
thwarting attempt at light*

*Don't play with my head
You are a master magician
whose wand torments and
taints all it contacts
bringing madness to all courtiers*

*I know it in my bones
It will be your turn
soon and madness
will generate new beginnings
and sweet enterprise*

What is the key we need that will help us to penetrate through to the truth of the lies that are being told by politicians over and over again and have been repeated for centuries? We need that something that opens and unlocks answers. We need that some small thing that will give us a sense of our own personal power and responsibility. We need something that will give us access to the darkest secrets of our own psyches and collectives that mindlessly destroy potential. A false sense of freedom or security cannot register sinister knowledge about the predator within us and outside of us.

Ask yourself what key you were forbidden to use in your experiences…the one that could have brought you to greater awareness? Was it education? The encouragement to ask questions? The ability to speak differently? Be sexually assertive? To stand alone? To discover your own truths and more?

Why do you think that the bride does not object to Bluebeard's mandate that she was not to use the small key? Perhaps you can identify with: I am getting so much; Things are good; I shouldn't rock the boat; I will really upset them. Obviously, she has been stripped of her instinct for curiosity and desire to look for what lies beneath his veneer. She replies, "Yes, sir. It is all quite fine".

If we "flesh" this statement, we might say, "It's okay" or "It suits me" or "It is satisfactory and reasonable". Ask yourself now what in **you** seduces you into saying, "It is all quite fine". Are you one to look at the pros only and disregard the cons? Do you honour the reasonable viewpoint versus your instincts? Are you lured easily by the promises of ease, increased security, the promise of elevated status in the eyes of your family, peers or boss?

In the tale of Bluebeard, the older sisters have the proper impulse towards consciousness. The youngest lacks curiosity and discernment. Emphasis on Nationhood and National Security strips us of this as does enmeshment with any system that discourages difference, authentic curiosity, freedom of speech or becomes withholding when someone dissents or asks for openness, honesty and direct communication.

The sisters whisper truth. They are open and alive, nosy, interested and awake to their curiosity. Feminine curiosity has been given a negative connotation in our culture. Women are seen as nosy while men are investigative. The kind of energy attached to the sisters in the tale is seen as natural, proper and constructive.

The function of the older sisters in terms of the development of the younger one is that they are her companions who support and encourage. Their wildest instincts are intact. They refuse to become compliant and complacent. This energy of the sisters is about the tics and nudges that one feels inside that remind us of what is important and true. If only we would listen!

What is your personal experience of coming up against a blank wall? What has twisted or tangled you that keeps you from knowing what you know down and deep inside? When have you set out to discover something and nothing comes up?

If you "flesh out" cellar, you might add to my list: dark; underground; bottom; foundation; dank; dirty things. From a political point of view: ulterior motives.

The blank wall in the story threatens to "fool the sisters". Other ways of making this statement might be: maybe I am making this up; maybe I am being too harsh; maybe I have misjudged. The captured and the naïve ones must learn to cut doors into walls that appear blank.

The "err..rrr" sound gets the women's attention. This is certainly a shift from what they see to what they hear now. Just as they were beginning to give up on one sense, the other comes to the rescue. We must use keen sensing, visual, auditory and kinesthetic. Our eyes, ears and sense of touch must become reliable sources of information to us. In this way, we are healing our instincts and our intuition and we will not suffer fools.

The two older sisters have been instinctive and impulsive all along. Once the door is opened, they confront the truth of Bluebeard's lies. They use a candle. Ask yourself now: Who or what has acted like a candles in the dark for you; Who or what has helped light the way for you?

Changed

Because of gender privilege
and your need to feel masculine
you saw a chance in me to
honour your father but
I had no idea that he
taught you to hate the me in you
and I have come to hate you
because of that

The subtleness of your tactics
blinded me to parts of myself that
at an earlier time had made me whole
Negated and reduced by the teachings
of my father…the Holy Father and you
I have lived outside of myself in your shadow
and I have come to hate you
because of that

The reclamation is nigh…in my best interest
I have my body my mind and now my spirit
that connect me to my early dreams
that had gone underground now ignited through
love, tenderness and care from one another
I have come to love you
for the lesson

Bluebeard has a ghastly history of mangling the feminine. Ask yourself, what has been mangled or murdered in **you** in light of the story?

The sisters slam the door and scream. The sign that remains with them is that they have seen the blood. If we were to "flesh out" blood now, we might come up with: life force; stains; death; sacrifice; evidence; emergency; essential to life. What can you add to the list?

The key itself keeps on bleeding. Once we have knowledge of something, then we have the responsibility to do something. Perhaps this is why so many keep their denial systems going. We would have to look at another angle and not remain victims railing against the world yet doing nothing about it. This is existential cowardice and borders on Evil. This blood is about the decimation of the deepest, most soulful aspects of creative life... a life lived not as much protectively as "correctively". It involves a personal willingness to embrace the truth and the responsibility to change patterns of behaviour that are destructive to the self, others and the world. This means that once we have seen, once we know something, we cannot ignore or pretend that it does not exist. What it also means is that you have to act and take personal responsibility in spite of what is deemed as acceptable or healthy. This is the consciousness that some have chosen to bravely seek and are ready to stand up for what they believe is truth at the time. Many have laid their lives on the line to do just that. I am speaking about conviction of the heart and not only the head. Our minds can fool us but when we are able to integrate the wisdom of the heart with the knowledge that we have accumulated, then we are in a position to defend what is right, just and noble. What means have you used to get rid of the "blood?" in other words, when have you destroyed evidence in order to deny the truth?

Depression

*There is a keeper
in my soul
that limits pain
and seeks resolve*

*It bespeaks
of gossamer days
and signals
respite in fortune*

*A script whips me into shape
and limits joy
that follows tears*

*There is angst
and death rattle
in this abnegation
that reaps dividends*

The dogged will to

flee sterility
and lame excuse
keeps me winded

I am in between
and that limbo
supplies the narcotic
that retards growth

The bride tries to put the key and the blood out of sight. She hopes it will go away or perhaps, that it all might have been a bad dream.

Bluebeard was enraged when he learned that his wife had discovered his evil. She failed the test of compliance and strict obedience to his word. She has complicated matters now. He does not have absolute control and power over her anymore. He cannot relate to her and so, he will kill her off. This is anti-life energy in the male. He is a wounded, or should I say a failed, magician in that he thought he knew enough about human behaviour to be able to manipulate. He does not know how to relate to the feminine on the inside as well as the outside. He is not capable of compassion and displays a lack of capacity in terms of being with any woman.

The bride has changed. She knows what to do. It is time for her to strengthen with the help of her wise sisters. She has to be able to contain the powerful emotions that will help her to take a stand against the predator and she has to work quietly because the sickest among us possess high instinct for the vulnerability of others. She will ready herself to accept the "brother" or the healthy masculine energy that will support her actions in the world. She asks that she be granted the time to make her peace with God and Bluebeard grants her fifteen minutes. She has chosen to move out of the place of being duped and "robotized" by someone who claimed to have her best interests at heart. She has to take good care of herself and grow up.

Dark Goddess

I met the Death Hag
She flashed her tainted teeth
With baited breath
I lay beneath her feet
"Sigh loudly Dear for they
won't know – those who think you dead for
in that soul lies
treasure bound in
black and gold and red
The stitches are loose the
chords run bare but in
that heart of yours there
is a mirror there.
What say you girl when looking in?"
She flashed a toothless smile

"A darkness deep and cheery yet
will bring a gift of fire
The flint a flame – the match is yours
please light it if you will
I'll keep you close and better yet
I'll hide beneath your smile"
So at her feet I laid my head
and moved at her command
With sinew jaw and claw unfurled
I let the blood run mad
My chest a drum, my heart beat time
*the rhythm **sturm und drang** or*
what's the word that says the thing
that means to come undone?
She comes and goes now and then
I know not when at all but
I feel her fierce and feisty there
as she hides beneath my smile

Bluebeard energy can never really be killed off. It must be transformed so that it can be of service in terms of available energy to get things done.

Just how do we do that? This has been my tenet at the beginning of this work. We are at a point in history where change is required at many levels, especially political. No longer should we suffer one country's subversive tactics as a way of undermining another nation's stability in order to better serve their own interests. As has been proven in the past, the supposed "puppet" turns out to be the "puppeteer" who, in turn, is the next target.

I urge you to be strong and carry the sword, to only use a knife with discernment as you use it to cut away to the truth by scraping through the debris that binds you and others to worn out paradigms that are no longer relevant or hold true. Take responsibility and pray as my grandmother did that all negative energy be extinguished and sent to the light for transformation so that it may be used for the greater good.

May we move to respect and support the development of each individual and culture so we do not make slave classes out of certain groups for the purpose of "scapegoating" and fooling ourselves into thinking that only an elite group have the right answers.

May we remember, lest we forget, that we are all one people on this "earthwalk"; here to find wholeness and not to achieve perfection.

Static brings change. The threshold experience of September 11, 2001 should serve to remind us that we are all accountable. I emphasize that it is about accountability and not blame. We must not get caught up in the beneficence of intent but rather, learn to value experience that gives knowledge and brings wisdom.

Understanding from "standing under" or from a place of subordination should never mean toleration. We spend too much time having to know about those in power and never come to know ourselves and our deepest convictions.

I respect our Canadian leader, Jean Chretien, for his decision not to support the war in Iraq, mainly because it shows that our leaders are reflecting the values of a country that is finally growing up and making its own decisions. We have decided to exit from the trap of shaming, blaming and laying guilt on others to do the dirty work that causes the decimation of nations that we need but will never respect.

How many of you are going to continue to support lies? Will you stand for the truth that we all need to become mature nations under the Creator?

I ask YOU?

EPILOGUE

It is Christmas time now and I sit listening to carols of old. I really listen this year as I meet the season in a different way from last year. My partner turns on the morning news this day of December 14th 2003 and I hear of the capture of Saddam Hussein; I stop everything now to listen, really listen.

This book sits waiting in my office for publication. I have not had the funds to start the process and I am left to wonder why I have been blocked in spite of trying to push ahead. I heard the carol, "I Wonder As I Wander" by Vanessa Williams as she passionately sings about why the savior, Jesus Christ came to die for poor lonely people like you and I. I find myself always working to understand that, in this lifetime, I am on a journey that has more to do with spiritual evolution than accumulation of material goods or fame. This keeps me hopeful. I want to believe that the abundance that I need is only in hiding and that there is something more to learn as I wait for the necessary funding. I struggle, especially in this season of my life, to contain an energy that makes me anxious and any form of relief comes only when I write down my ideas. Sometimes I want to roll over in my bed and never wake up as the responsibility that I feel to be in service to humankind seems more than I can handle. I understand now what Christ meant when He asked His Father to let "this cup pass from Me". I am, at this very moment, trying to get rid of a line showing up on my computer screen that says 'human resources department' and wondering where on earth it came from? As suddenly as it appeared, it is now gone – maybe this is a sign I need to continue in spite of my tiredness. I am reminded of one Christmas morning only three years ago. I was struggling once again to find enough money to eat and survive when the phone rang . There was no answer on the other end of the line but when I checked the message recorder it had transcribed, "the good shepherd" and I became chilled with what I interpreted as some kind of further direction or, more likely, support to continue my work of helping others to discover their innate divinity.

I returned to the television to catch the latest information from CNN. What I witnessed on the screen was an old man struggling to keep his mouth open while an American doctor searched and probed it. He then pointed to areas on his head where fleas might be feeding. The picture flashed on

76

the screen over and over again. It was Saddam Hussein who had been discovered in a crawl space which the newscasters later referred to as a spider hole. I felt nauseous and angry while the free world was showing signs of celebration. It was a sobering reality for me and perhaps to others who have begun to look behind the veils of illusion at this time in the history of the world. Just who is the country rat and who is the city rat and where does the difference lie?

Now I know why the book is on hold. I believe another piece had to come together for me before publication.

The holidays, or, should I say, holy days are upon us again. I hear President Bush say in his address to the nation that now that Hussein has been captured, a dark and painful era is over. I know that most of us would like to think so but all I saw today was a tired human being who was captured. We have a lot more dark and ugly things to look at before the painful era is over. It is my belief that when we are suffering, we need to look at what is truly missing in our lives and I have spoken of that in the previous chapters of this book. Capture of the scapegoat never means that the reign of terror is over. **Remember: the victims hold the most power and lure the rescuers.** These rescuers will get "set-up" in the dynamic to abandon themselves and are blamed if they are not in total complicity with the victim. This is the addiction to "power-over" which continues to perpetuate itself unless someone, or in this case, some nations, have the courage of conviction and integrity to exit from the game and be willing to be labeled as villain or traitor even though that is not the truth. Remember the story of Bluebeard and the skeletons in his closet? Well, the Americans have shown us Saddam Hussein but I believe that he is not the skeleton in the closet that most of us would like to believe. Remember also, that at the beginning of this book, I said that there would be no miracles in terms of solutions to world's problems at this point in time. The villain/victim/ rescuer game is only a diversion from the real issues. What we need is more accountability.

Personally, I have moved beyond the naïve maiden and dutiful daughter of the culture and the punishing Father God to becoming a woman who has looked and seen. I have become dissident in terms of poisonous prescriptions of a culture also gone mad with power and I am willing to be dangerous to the status quo. I am a changing woman and a defender of a faith in evolution, co-creation and passion.

The true theme of Christmas is about miraculous rebirth, beauty and light as we make our way through the darkest time of the year. Through the darkness comes the light and celebration is about making it through and not around it. We all need scapegoats when we are cowardly in terms of accepting truth even when it is in our faces and I fear that today, another puppeteer who was once only a puppet has been the source of celebration. This is the dark night for the world as we continue to be duped into believing that evil is perpetuated by only the few; especially women, children, minority groups and some men.

I ask you, can you make the leap and embrace the need for a rebirth that is occurring in us all? Humanity needs to move into more actualization of innate divine potential and not into the amassing of arms, the emphasis on gross national product and winning violent power games.

Our babies are angels and most of them are now born into a fallen world. Everyday through the media, we see them suffering all over the globe. What have we come to when we continue to use and abuse, nation over nation, political party over political party, men over women and children?. ..and the beat goes on…

I believe that our true mission in this holy time is to reclaim the lost parts of ourselves, to move from 'brokenness' to fullness within this violent realm. Please don't dismiss me as utopian yet.

Imagine that a miracle can unfold. **We** need a miracle and the real issue is not whether God is capable of working one but whether or not **we** are. **We** need a shift in perception. **We** need to move from required atonement as **we** conceive into the world and emphasize "at-one-ment". I am asking you to conceive of embracing the extraordinary in all that lives!

What if we believed that we were all begotten children of the Creator who represents a masculine face as well as a feminine face? In this morass that we find ourselves in politically and morally, is it not the time for the critical mass to believe that the Creator is interested in happiness and not suffering? After all, time and space are only illusion. It is only through mental 'miscreation' and "stinking thinking" that we become separated from each other, the earth and all of its creatures. As long as we base our perceptions on that plane "of difference", there will be no salvation for us or the planet. We are staring at the horrors of this central political and religious tenet that permeates our cultures. When did it all start – this knot around our hearts? I have referred to my beliefs in the text of this work. I believe that "at-one-ment" and the need to correct our perceptions on a causal level is our only form of salvation. This is about seeing ourselves not as separate from each other because of gender, colour or, race. Once even one of us can see beyond the veils of illusion, nothing will be the same on the planet. The old order of hierarchical construct, or perhaps better called the testosterone imperative, is vicious world-wide today only because its days are numbered. Perhaps this is where Saddam finds himself today! But where is Osama Bin Laden? … He is everywhere…Remember!

The young are already trying to move into a new sensibility. They are hungry for the language of spiritual development, not the language of oppression and winning at all costs. This need is manifesting itself in depression, anxiety, eating disorders, attention deficit disorders, rage and suicide. It is a split screen for our youth where domination and brute force is extant and insidious in the one hand, and on the other, a sensibility that is stronger than ever because of a new consciousness that is struggling to make itself known.

I am listening to the carol, "What Child is This?" and stop to ponder as this year I listen even more intently to the lyrics, "who laid to rest on Mary's lap is sleeping" and "the virgin sings her lullaby". I am even more convinced that the world is in need if a fuller integration of feminine values. I don't believe that masculine values in and of themselves are the problem. It is, rather, the distortion of them over the centuries of entrenchment of Christian patriarchy which has its origin in Greek vernacular meaning father (pater) rule (archien). It has come to mean a way of social organization marked by the authority or supremacy of men and fathers. Western civilization has been organized this way since pre-history but it is now showing signs of real demise at this moment in time. To see it as a "wounder" of feminine life is not easy and it is so familiar and pervasive, let alone insidious, in our lives. We have come to accept that the widespread attitudes and effects of patriarchy are a "given" and they are so woven into our culture that most of us think that is what reality is! It is only one way of viewing reality and most of us have bought into it. We must see it clearly and recognize that it has been embedded in our psyches. This view has been passed on as the natural, divinely created order of life. It is about the subtle ingraining of hierarchy as natural by the church, family, marriage, workplace, politics and all kinds of systems of thought. With men at the top or entitled to being on top, and women and children below, a way of relating was put into place based on dominance and dependence. The consequence is that the role of the one above is to dominate and oversee the ones below. The role of the ones below is to answer to and depend upon the one above. The one above then has to protect his prestigious place at the top. He learns to stay up by putting others below and keeping them down and struggling to be content with the way things are to simply survive.

Hierarchy issues forth a whole series of power relations. God as Father rules over the Church, Holy Fathers rule over the churches, clergy fathers over laity, males over females, husbands over wives. The beat goes on in that this pattern extends to our relationship to nature and how countries seek dominance over each other.

I heard the reporters state today that Saddam Hussein had been an abused child. Haven't we all been used and abused in and by a hierarchical political system? **Remember** that the sisters in the 'Bluebeard tale' had a naïve mother who colluded in the demise of her own daughter; she was not grounded enough in her own wisdom and sense of herself to protect her child from a violent man. We live in a violent world where the head has been separated from the heart. We have been taught reverence for thought over consideration of the heart and the body's inherent wisdom. What if, in his youth, Saddam had been acknowledged by his father and those around him for his leadership qualities, his tenacity, his intelligence, natural charisma and compassion? The schoolyard bully is often an abused child who compensates for insecurity by scaring the 'bejeesus' out of the vulnerable. The sickest among us do possess high intuition for the vulnerable. This sickness, I believe, has more to do with a sick politic than it has to do with genetics and geography.

Revenge seems to be the mandate of the powerful who need to control what is not theirs to control. When someone has been victimized, they may want to get back at a significant person in their life and this may be manifested through illness, accidents, conflicts and problems created. This is a dynamic which is a significant form of communication and attack on another or others. The message at a subconscious level is, "This happened because of you" or "It would not have happened if you...". This is victim psychology and requires the aforementioned "scapegoating clause" in their contract.

The essence of the victim stance is, "I am willing to be hurt so I can hurt you". Most of us who are into revenge would feel embarrassed to find that this dynamic operates inside of us. Actively trying to hurt someone else because of the pain that one might be suffering never works. Responsible living requires that one goes through the pain of accepting his/her own truth and not try to hurt another or others to end the pain. Often the problems that we suffer have more to do with avenging oneself on another. Here the personal and the political are not so disparate. The question that power mongers might formulate is, "Who am I really trying to get back at by having this problem occur?" or, "What hidden agenda is behind my actions or these problems?"

Becoming aware of what is really going on is half the battle and most of us are used to avoiding this kind of personal and collective responsibility. To really be free we must be willing to give up the suffering and the accusations that go with it; sometimes in the name of God! This behaviour would be empowering in that we could move forward and, in coming to a new level of openness, receive something that we have always wanted. How many in power positions in the world are still operating from a place of trying to prove something to their fathers at a subconscious level? Are Saddam Hussein, George Bush and many others in places of power not equals in this stance? I ask you. Dictatorship comes in many guises.

The acid test that assures we are beyond revenge is that we are no longer suffering. We are a world in pain and into crucifying the Earth Mother with our ridiculous war games. Revenge and using scapegoats has never worked and it stops us from the joy of truly living. Isn't it time that all of humankind accepts these hidden dynamics as to what is really going on? We need to forgive and let go so that we can all become truly healed. True forgiveness comes not in the forgetting but through the full remembrance of the wrongs including feeling the grief that comes with the process. Only then can we begin the letting go. When we continue to fill our psychic spaces with revenge and resentment towards our trespassers then we are giving them power over us and we have not forgiven ourselves.

As I bring closure to this book, I feel I have to emphasize that we need to formulate questions and not operate in blind faith believing that the "powerful" in terms of "power over" and the "hierarchical constructivists" have everyone's best interests at heart. After the first abandonment there is no other and the only one who can abandon you now is yourself. This realization comes with mature vision.

Ask yourself the question: What holds me back in my own life? There are things and dark places within ourselves, places that we keep fighting and refuse to bring to the light of consciousness. Ask yourself: Is this way of operating serving me? The old order lives inside of each of us and there is truly no security in creating the same. Have you noticed imbalance internally as well as externally where competition, logic, objectivity, and matters of the head have found prominence over concerns of relatedness, inclusiveness, and matters of the heart?

Lest Christians forget, Christ was of woman born. Have you noticed imbalance in the way that dogma, theological rightness, triumph of the Christian way, oratorical sermons, church business, nationalism, individual pursuit, conversion figures and breaking scripture down into various hermenuetics or interpretations have frequently been valued over feelings, tears and peace?

Liberation is about melting "in". Sit quietly now and ask your higher Self to show you what you are not seeing. It may come to you in a dream if you pay attention. Ask for guidance and discover a new way to pray for the grace to walk the path of higher truth.

We pay a price when we do not take responsibility and resign ourselves to, "I cannot change it" or, "It is all too overwhelming". **We just have to begin**. Awareness is the first step. We are always finding ourselves at the threshold of new beginnings when we accept that death is a constant and the price we pay for living. We can learn to become comfortable with the death aspect of life as we become more comfortable with ending outmoded ways of being, politics, relationships that no longer serve us and changes in perspective. As we shine more light on situations and work towards change and personal development, we realize that we can change at the personal level. The outmoded politics of cultures gone mad with power will alter. We need to be able to say, "I can rise above this though I did not cause it". When all is held in this perspective, the inner and outer worlds align. Consciousness has to be there and it will attract the necessary abundance. The problem with the modern world is that we have not grown enough to genuinely conceive and the world is a fantasy gone amuck. At a certain point we have to ask: have we become addicted to suffering? Happiness is really not such a bad thing. We all contribute more and do more good if we are happy. When our "own life" is handled we know the joy of the gift of life. When we are stuck in "survival mentality", which is where most of the world seems to be, then we worry mostly about the material plane. Our creativity must be unleashed for the world to thrive. There is nothing more powerful than the agreement that all can be wonderful in "my life". May this be the gift to yourself this Christmas and always. Let "I am living in joy" be your mantra.

I invite you to accept the Creator's gift of life, love and joy for yourself and, by doing that, it will lift the entire world.

The majority of human consciousness will "rise up" and ascend – all else will drop away. This is the magic of this threshold or "liminal" time. We must learn, I believe, that we are greater than our problems. This is truly the "higher love" that we aspire to unconsciously. I ask you to bring this human need to consciousness; we are all hungry for this kind of love and no single human being can contain these projections just as they cannot contain our evil projections. Perhaps it is time for the "Second Coming" that so many wait for. This is the time for the coming of a "cosmic Christ" consciousness in each of us. When we infuse spirit into our own life we will stop the plodding along and plugging into others to save us from ourselves. Think of the extraordinary creative tension that exists versus random stress and living someone else's vision. This is the true nature of Christmas and the Christ can be born in you. Go into your closet or spider hole and see who is really there. Something good and beautiful is about to emerge. Look at what is possible for you and all of humankind.

I heard about the response of many countries of the world in terms of Saddam's capture today. I did not hear Canada mentioned. Has she been dismissed? It is my hope that our subsequent leaders will continue to support our Canadian values spawned by our increasingly urban and post - modern pluralist cultures as Jean Chretien has done. Post - 9/11 Canadians have developed a profoundly different view of the world than Americans. We have been re-Canadianized by our leader's decision to sit out on the war in Iraq. Not sending troops there because we were already committed to Afghanistan wasn't in keeping with our traditions. Canada, along with many nations, was awaiting the United Nations sanction for invading Iraq rather than act on one country's single-mindedness. We have not been pacifists. Our country went to the two great wars ahead of America and joined the Korean War. The test to most Canadian leaders has been to assert independence from Britain and lately, Canada is taking her place in the world and it is my hope that we do not find ourselves crawling back to subservience and killing innocents. Our mandate has been to preserve justice and fairness for all and not disregard rule of law at home in the name of fighting terrorism. We must not let ourselves be dismissed easily.

Will you dismiss what I have to say? How much structure or stricture will **you** need to impose on a free-flow of ideas? I ask **you!**

BIBLIOGRAPHY

The following are among the books which influenced me in the process of completing this work.

Borysenko, Joan. "A Woman's Journey to God. Finding the Feminine Path". New York, N.Y: Riverhead Books, 1999

Fox, Matthew. "The Coming of the Cosmic Christ". New York, N.Y: Harper Collins, 1998

Kushner, Harold S. "How Good Do We Have To BE? A New Understanding of Guilt and Forgiveness". Boston, New York, London, Toronto: Little, Brown and Company, 1996

Pinkola Estes, Clarissa. "Women Who Run With The Wolves". New York, N.Y: Ballantine Books, 1992

Williamson, Marianne. "A Return To Love". New York, N.Y: Harper Collins, 1992

Woodman, Marion. "Leaving My Father's House: A Journey To Conscious Femininity" (with Kate Dawson, Mary Hamilton and Rita Greer Allen). Boston: Shambhala, 1992

ABOUT THE AUTHOR

Sandra C. Johnston is a certified counsellor with the Canadian Guidance and Counselling Association and holds a Bachelor of Arts degree in English and Psychology, a Bachelor of Education degree in English Literature and Drama and a Masters of Education degree in Counselling Psychology.

She is an Internationally registered Somatic Movement Therapist and Psychotherapist in private practice. She works with individuals and groups where she combines traditional psychotherapeutic intervention with the creative therapies. This unique approach has helped her to facilitate healing in her clients at body – mind – spirit levels of being. She also draws on her own experience as a teacher of Drama, English, Creative Writing, Music and Dance.

She is the author of "In Her Own Time: A Woman's Journey To Self" and currently has several other works in process.

www.sandrajohnston.com

**Information on workshops, Groups
and seminars**

To sponsor a Workshop, Seminar or Retreat in your area, please contact Sandra C. Johnston at:

Sandra Johnston
c/o Morgaine Publishing
1-57 Victoria Ave.
Chatham, ON N7L 2Z9

Ph: 519-355-1017

Additional information can be found on Sandra's web site www. sandrajohnston.com

Printed in the United States
20596LVS00005B/1-138

9 781418 431921